feed your chakras

Recipes to Restore & Balance
Your Energy Centers

tiffany la forge

wellfleet
press

table of contents

Mains

Snacks & Treats

introduction

Welcome. I'm thrilled you're here.

Whether you are completely new to the concept of chakras or no stranger to the subject, you are in the right place. Supporting your energy centers and adopting a more mindful approach to overall well-being can benefit anyone.

When you think of supporting the seven chakras, what comes to mind first? Likely it's a combination of yoga, meditation, breathwork, crystals, essential oils, and energy healing. While these are all important, I am here to propose that one of the easiest and most powerful ways to balance, unblock, and support the chakras is through nourishing foods.

Science has revealed that everything, including us, is fundamentally made up of energy. Since the seven chakras are the main energy centers of the body—governing our physical, mental, and spiritual livelihood—it makes sense that they would be sustained by the very means through which our bodies obtain energy: food.

As a seasoned professional chef for the better part of my life, there is one thing I undeniably understand, and that's the significance of food. What we eat, how we eat, and where our food comes from all have a direct impact on our health, energy levels, and overall well-being. Food is a universal language that connects us to Earth and to each other.

You've likely heard the importance of "eating the rainbow" and including a variety of colorful foods in your daily diet. This idea resonates here, and we will explore this deeper and how it connects to our body's energy centers. The phytochemicals responsible for providing foods with color—from rich red to vibrant violet— also provide a host of antioxidants, health benefits, and powerful protection from disease.

As a professional chef and health writer, I combine the idea of supporting chakra centers with science-backed data on food and nutrition. I believe that you should take great care of not only your physical health but also your mental health. This book focuses on a mindful, holistic, and creative approach to enhance well-being and balance the seven chakras.

Whether you are looking to heal a certain chakra, balance your overall energy, or simply incorporate more whole foods into your daily life, this book is for you. You will learn attainable, delicious, and beautiful recipes that are rich in vivid natural colors and nutrients. You will explore how to work with your energy centers and use them to release what no longer serves you. You will discover how to employ the chakras to create your most balanced and vibrant life.

The content and recipes found in this book will nourish the body, soul, and mind. That's how powerful I believe food is.

Food is culture, love, connection, and joy.
It is healing.
This is Feed Your Chakras.

PART I

chakras 101

Understanding the Seven Energy Centers

The concept of chakras originates from ancient Indian spiritual traditions and is defined as the main energy centers within the human body. Translating into "spinning wheel," the seven main chakras are located along the spine, from the base of the spine to the crown of the head. Each chakra corresponds to vital organs and areas of the body that may affect both physical and emotional well-being. Balancing or unblocking the chakras is believed to promote harmony within the body, mind, and spirit.

The seven main chakras are as follows:

 root chakra (muladhara): The first chakra, located at the base of the spine, is associated with stability, security, and feeling grounded. It is represented by the color red and the element earth.

 sacral chakra (svadhisthana): The second chakra, situated just below the navel, is connected to creativity, emotional expression, and sensuality. It is represented by the color orange and the element of water.

 solar plexus chakra (manipura): The third chakra, located in the lower abdomen, is linked to personal power, confidence, and identity. It is represented by the color yellow and the element of fire.

 heart chakra (anahata): The fourth chakra, positioned in the center of the chest, is associated with love, compassion, and connection. It is represented by the color green and the element of air.

 throat chakra (vishuddha): The fifth chakra, found in the throat region, is related to communication, self-expression, and authenticity. It is represented by the color blue and the element of ether (space).

 third eye chakra (ajna): The sixth chakra, located in the center of the forehead, is associated with intuition, imagination, and inner wisdom. It is represented by the color indigo and the element of light.

 crown chakra (sahasrara): The seventh chakra, situated at the crown of the head, signifies spiritual connection, higher consciousness, and enlightenment. It is represented by the color violet or white and the element of thought.

I think of chakras as a powerful blueprint for overall well-being, personal growth, and self-care. Working with and balancing these energy points can facilitate and open up new pathways to wellness and healing. Perhaps you want to be more creative, learn to set boundaries, reduce your stress and anxiety levels, or simply strengthen your mind-body connection. Or maybe you wish to find higher truths and understanding by enhancing your intuition, spiritual growth, or inner peace. Whatever journey you are on, chances are very likely that chakra work can help in some way.

Although this book emphasizes using food to balance your chakras, you will find many other tips to heal and harmonize your energy. My unique perspective—as a culinary professional, health and wellness writer, and certified chakra energy healer—has made me realize the profound power that food has in relation to all aspects of wellness. This includes physical, mental, and emotional health. To reiterate a saying I am sure you've heard many times, I believe we are what we eat.

All of the nutrition information in this book is backed by science, as there are copious amounts of research on food and proven health benefits. While scientific research on chakras is lacking, some of the most significant work in relation to this was done by Dr. Valerie Hunt, a scientist and UCLA professor who studied human energy fields and the interactions with health and consciousness. When it comes to the topic of food, she found that consuming fruits, vegetables, whole grains, and seeds enhanced human energy fields, while eating processed foods made someone's energy field dull and lifeless.

The recipes in this book focus on balance and highlight whole foods vibrant in the colors of the rainbow. Foods rich in nutrients, phytochemicals, antioxidants, omega-3 fatty acids, protein, and fiber will balance and energize the body and the chakras while protecting against disease.

Next, let's delve deeper into each of the seven chakras and learn how we can balance them.

root chakra

sanskrit name
MULADHARA

location
BASE OF SPINE
(TAILBONE/PELVIC FLOOR)

color
RED

element
EARTH

characteristics
SECURITY, STABILITY,
GROUNDEDNESS,
SURVIVAL, STRENGTH,
PURPOSE

When discussing the order of chakras, we start with the first chakra, known as the root chakra, located at the base of the spine.

If we imagine our body as a house or structure, the *muladhara* chakra functions as the foundation, providing essential support and stability to keep our home standing strong. Closely connected to its element earth, this chakra plays a pivotal role in keeping us grounded, rooted, and secure. It is only natural that the root chakra is our first chakra, as it serves as the very basis for our energetic system and the foundation upon which everything else is built.

I like to summarize the key characteristics of the root chakra using four powerful "S" words: stability, security, survival, and strength. When this chakra is balanced, these are all fulfilled. You will experience a sense of stability and security in your foundation, enabling you to face challenges with confidence and trust that your needs will be met. You will also experience a sense of alignment with your purpose and values. Conversely, if your root chakra is blocked or unbalanced, you may experience feelings of fear, threat, and instability.

This chakra also has strong connections to family relations, a sense of belonging, survival, and fundamental necessities such as food, water, and shelter. Individuals who have grown up in circumstances where their basic needs weren't met often encounter challenges with this chakra. Similarly, financial worries can also impede the balance of this chakra and give rise to emotions of fear and insecurity.

A blocked root chakra can manifest in various ailments such as anxiety, depression, loneliness, low self-esteem, digestive issues, weight changes, lethargy, and pelvic or abdominal pain.

As someone who has dealt with a lifelong anxiety disorder, I have encountered significant difficulties with this specific chakra. Anxiety is an emotion that all humans experience, from worrying about the future to feeling fearful in certain situations. Anxiety, whether it is clinical or general, has a common trait: It generates feelings of fear, danger, insecurity, and instability—all of which stand in stark contrast to a balanced root chakra state.

Maybe you're familiar with anxious feelings as well, especially over the past few years. According to the World Health Organization, the COVID-19 pandemic triggered a 25 percent increase in cases of anxiety and depression worldwide. A pandemic, economic recession, or war are examples of extreme cases where this chakra would be challenged. However, there are many occurrences that can affect the muladhara's energy, from the loss of a job to unhealed past trauma to family issues.

Thankfully, there are several ways in which we can work on balancing the root chakra. Let's cultivate a sense of inner safety and nurture our own strength, stability, and purpose.

feeding your root chakra

To nourish and balance our root chakra, we primarily focus on consuming protein-rich foods, root vegetables, and foods that are rich in the color red.

protein

The body needs three macronutrients—protein, fat, and carbohydrates—to function properly and provide energy. Out of these, protein is particularly crucial for nourishing the root chakra. It plays a vital role in building physical strength by aiding in the repair and maintenance of muscle tissue through its amino acids.

Proteins, often called the "workhorses" of cells, are the fundamental building blocks of the human body. They provide structural support to our cells and are among the most active molecules found in all living organisms. This makes sense why the root chakra—which centers around structure, strength, and foundation— would benefit from such a powerful and fundamental nutrient like protein.

Due to the muladhara's red color, which signifies the earth, clay, and blood, many find red meat particularly grounding for this chakra. However, quality protein can be found in many sources, including plants, grains, legumes, and seeds. Animal proteins are "complete" proteins, which means they contain the nine essential amino acids our body can't produce on its own. While there are some complete plant-based proteins (quinoa, buckwheat, and soy, for example), most are not. However, eating a balanced diet focused on a variety of protein-rich foods, whether animal or plant-based, will nourish and energize both the body and the first chakra.

Eight Ways to Get More Protein

- Cook rice and grains in bone broth instead of water.

- Add protein powder to your smoothies, baked goods, oatmeal, energy bites, and soups.

- Add collagen creamer to your morning coffee.

- When choosing yogurt, opt for high-protein Greek yogurt.

- Cook with protein-packed pastas such as red lentil, edamame, and chickpea pasta.

- Include protein with every meal.

- For convenience, have some ready-to-go options at hand, such as protein bars, energy bites, hard-boiled eggs, canned tuna, jerky, and protein bento boxes.

- Give salads a protein boost with grilled chicken, fish, edamame, chopped nuts, or hemp seeds.

root vegetables

For our next root chakra food, we take note of the muladhara's element: earth. Root vegetables—such as beets, carrots, and potatoes—grow beneath the ground and are nourished by Earth's soil.

I love root vegetables so much that I named my blog after one (*Parsnips and Pastries*). When I think of root vegetables, I think of survival, sturdiness, and resilience, all words that deeply resonate with this chakra. These hardy crops are securely grounded in the earth and most can withstand some pretty harsh conditions. In fact, such conditions often make these vegetables better. Take the parsnip or carrot, for instance, which becomes the most flavorful when exposed to near-freezing winter temperatures for an extended period of time. This converts the starches in the vegetable into sugar and gives it a sweeter flavor profile.

But the importance of where root vegetables grow goes beyond just their location. Growing underground allows these vegetables to absorb various nutrients from the soil, such as carotenoids, potassium, fiber, and vitamin C. One of the biggest benefits of root vegetables is their high antioxidant content due to their abundance of phenols and flavonoids.

red foods

Naturally, we must also include red foods in our list of root chakra supporters because the energy of this grounding chakra resonates with the color red.

First, let's discuss what actually makes red food *red*. Red fruits and vegetables have the phytochemicals lycopene and anthocyanins to thank for their powerful, bold color. Lycopene, a plant pigment found within the carotenoids family, is known as one of the most potent natural antioxidants. Research has found that lycopene offers protection against certain types of cancers and contributes to the overall health of the heart, brain, and eyes.

Anthocyanins, another antioxidant found in red foods, offers similar cancer-fighting properties in addition to possessing antidiabetic, anti-inflammatory, and antimicrobial effects.

Many argue that red meat or red beans (which are both sources of protein and red foods) and beets (which is both a root vegetable and a red food) are the ultimate supporters of the first chakra.

list of root chakra foods

Animal-Based Proteins
Beef
Cheese
Eggs
Fish
Kefir
Milk
Poultry
Seafood
Wild game
Yogurt

Plant-Based Proteins
Beans
Buckwheat
Green peas
Lentils
Nutritional yeast
Nuts
Oats
Quinoa
Seeds
Soy-based protein
 (tofu, tempeh, edamame)
Spelt
Spirulina
Wild rice

Root Vegetables
Beet
Carrot
Cassava
Celery root
Daikon
Garlic
Ginger
Horseradish
Jerusalem artichoke
Jicama
Kohlrabi
Leek
Onion
Parsnip
Potato
Radish
Rutabaga
Shallot
Sweet potato
Turmeric
Turnip
Yam

Red Foods
Apple
Beet
Blood orange
Cayenne pepper
Cherries
Chile pepper
Cranberries
Goji berries
Kidney beans
Paprika
Pink grapefruit
Plum
Pomegranate
Radish
Raspberries
Red bell pepper
Red cabbage
Red currants
Red grapes
Red meat
Red onion
Red-skinned potato
Rhubarb
Strawberries
Tomato
Watermelon

Other
Hibiscus tea
Mushroom
Red wine

root chakra meal plan examples

	Breakfast	Lunch	Dinner	Snack
MONDAY	Build-Your-Own Savory Breakfast Bowls (page 114)	Bone Broth Gazpacho (page 121)	Grounding Beef and Mushroom Stew (page 154)	Baked Beet Chips with Labneh Za'atar Dip (page 179)
TUESDAY	Cinnamon Apple Quinoa Porridge (page 110)	Hearty Vegetarian Chili (page 158)	Sheet Pan Chicken Thighs with Roasted Root Vegetables (page 141)	Strawberry Rhubarb Crisp (page 180)
WEDNESDAY	Protein-Packed Root Vegetable Hash (page 108)	Spinach salad with grilled chicken, roasted beets, chickpeas, goat cheese, and balsamic vinaigrette	Turkey Picadillo Stuffed Peppers (page 156)	Red apple rounds topped with nut butter and pomegranate seeds
THURSDAY	Chocolate Cherry Chia Pudding (page 106)	Cobb salad with turkey bacon and yogurt-based dressing	Tofu or shrimp stir-fry	Protein bento boxes with hard-boiled eggs, turkey, red bell pepper, red grapes, and hummus
FRIDAY	Egg omelet with red peppers, onion, and Cheddar cheese, served with turkey bacon and strawberries	Vegetable and lentil soup	Mexican-style stuffed sweet potatoes with black beans, quinoa, and pico de gallo	Protein smoothie

root chakra crystals

Use the following crystals to absorb negative energy, ground you, and provide security and strength to support the root chakra:

 black obsidian It is believed that the mirror-like qualities of this rich black stone show you the truth of your own soul. Like all black stones, obsidian is protective and grounding and can help you release what no longer serves you.

 garnet This beautiful red stone offers a high vibration and helps you trust your instincts (including your survival instincts), promotes passion, and purges negative energy from the body. It is a beneficial crystal for both the first and second chakras.

 hematite Hematite, one of the most abundant minerals in Earth's surface and shallow crust, is a calming and balancing stone helpful in keeping you grounded.

 red jasper A widely sought-after protection stone, red jasper offers numerous benefits, such as overcoming challenges, boosting motivation, and nurturing inner strength.

 ruby This stunning red stone helps connect to the earth and aids in security, providing a greater sense of stability in yourself and the world around you. Ruby is also very beneficial for the heart chakra, so choose this stone if you have issues with both your first and your fourth chakra.

root chakra yoga poses

Practice the following root chakra yoga poses to help you regain and build strength, connect to the earth, and promote balance and stability:

tree pose (vrksasana) Tree pose is a balancing and strengthening pose that can help you feel rooted and confident. To practice this pose, begin by balancing on one leg and pressing the foot of the other leg against the inner thigh (or calf or ankle for modification) of the standing leg. Extend your arms upward with your palms touching. Hold this position for 30 seconds, then switch legs to repeat the same pose.

child's pose (balasana) Child's pose is a relaxing and grounding position that allows you to feel supported, connected, and safe. To practice this pose, kneel on the floor and sit back on your heels. Spread your knees about as wide as your hips and touch your big toes together. Bring your chest down to the ground and surrender to the weight of your body. Rest your forehead on the floor and keep your arms either at your sides or extended in front of you.

easy pose (sukhasana) This peaceful pose allows you to feel supported by the earth beneath you and is a great position for practicing meditation. To practice this pose, sit in a comfortable position with your legs crossed in front of you. Bring your arms down to your sides and let your palms rest gently on top of your knees or in your lap.

garland pose (malasana) This deep squat activates the pelvic floor, improves circulation to the abdominal organs and pelvis, and opens up the root chakra. To practice this pose, begin by standing with your feet slightly wider than your hips. Bend your knees and lower your hips until they are just above the floor, while widening your feet as necessary. Then, bring your palms together in a prayer position and press your elbows against your knees.

mountain pose (tadasana) Mountain pose, the foundation of all standing yoga poses, can benefit body awareness, posture, stability, and strength. To practice this pose, stand with your feet together and your arms relaxed at your sides, palms facing forward. Evenly balance your weight through the bottom four corners of each foot and feel firmly rooted to the earth. Keep your leg muscles engaged and your upper body lengthened and tall.

root chakra affirmations

I feel firmly rooted in my life.

I am safe.

I belong.

I am grounded.

I am strong and empowered.

I am connected to my body.

I feel at home wherever I am.

I feel secure in my place in life.

I am exactly where I need to be.

I am capable of providing myself with my basic needs.

I have all the necessary tools to succeed.

I am aligned with my purpose.

I can establish meaningful connections with my community and my family, whether they are biological or chosen.

The earth provides me with support and nourishment.

I have the necessary support to successfully navigate difficult situations.

Even when the world around me feels chaotic, I can remain grounded and calm.

more ways to support the root chakra

essential oils Grounding essential oils such as red spikenard, vetiver, frankincense, cedarwood, black pepper, and patchouli support the first chakra.

earthing Try grounding, also called "earthing," to support this chakra. This practice physically connects your body with the earth and can be done by walking barefoot, lying on the ground, or using grounding mats. Grounding has been scientifically shown to reduce inflammation, pain, and stress.

nature Spending time in nature is vital for nurturing the first chakra. It's not limited to practicing grounding; you can also go hiking, have a meal at the park, or experience forest bathing, which involves immersing yourself in the sights and sounds of your natural surroundings.

gardening Gardening is a form of grounding that can also promote a healthy, balanced relationship with the foods you consume. Try planting your own root vegetables or tomatoes, or visit a local farm to take a class or tour.

eating with your hands Many cultures eat with their hands and doing so can create a more mindful, sensual, and connected experience with your food.

sharing meals with others Since the root chakra resonates with familial relations and community, share or cook a meal with others to feed the muladhara.

sacral chakra

sanskrit name
SVADHISTHANA

location
BELOW THE NAVEL,
PERINEUM

color
ORANGE

element
WATER

characteristics
SENSUALITY, SEXUALITY,
PASSION, CREATIVITY,
EMOTIONS, SELF-EXPRESSION

Svadhisthana, the Sanskrit name for the second chakra, has a few different translations: "sweetness," "one's own dwelling place," and "sacred home for the self."

The sacral chakra does indeed represent the sweetness in life, including passion, sensuality, emotions, and creativity. This chakra is built upon what gives life richness, pleasure, and joy. Some believe this chakra is governed by Parvati, the Hindu goddess of fertility and devotion.

Since water is the sacral chakra's element, this chakra closely aligns with the "flow" of life and ability to accept and embrace change. When the second chakra is balanced, you will feel inspired and creative. This can translate into anything from creating art to coming up with new ideas for a business to cooking. You will also be able to express yourself, keep your emotions and relationships in balance, and feel like you have a healthy connection with your sexuality.

On the contrary, a blocked or underactive svadhisthana may manifest in feelings of repression, lack of inspiration, dissatisfaction with life, and low libido. An imbalanced sacral chakra can also create feelings of emotional instability, which may mean being too sensitive to emotions (intense emotional ups and downs or mood swings) or not in tune with your emotions at all (detachment or disconnection).

In addition to balancing the second chakra with the following foods, we can focus on not only *what* we eat but also *how* we eat. This chakra focuses on your relationships—with yourself, with others, and with food.

We can concentrate on the latter by not only feeding our body with nourishing foods, but also by taking joy and pleasure in cooking and eating. Create your own recipes, experiment with new ingredients, visit farmers markets, cook with intention, and don't be afraid to "play" with your food. That is exactly what professional chefs do—we use plates as a canvas to create beautiful compositions full of complementary colors and textures to delight all of the senses.

Let's find joy and spark creativity as we feed our sacral chakra.

feeding your sacral chakra

To nourish and harmonize our sacral chakra, we focus on incorporating foods rich in omega-3s, hydrating liquids, and tropical fruits. Additionally, we can balance this chakra with foods that support sexual health and foods that are vibrant in orange hues.

healthy fats and omega-3-rich foods

Healthy fats nourish and sustain the body in a variety of ways. Fats provide the body with energy and help absorb nutrients such as vitamins A, D, E, and K. Additionally, fats promote satiety, or the feeling of being full. Omega-3 fatty acids are especially helpful for cellular function and the second chakra. Research studies have proven that these fats reduce inflammation, promote brain health, protect against heart disease, and more.

When we discuss healthy fats, we are referring to unsaturated fats. Unsaturated fats are liquid at room temperature in oil form and are also found in certain solid foods. Examples of these fats include olive oil, vegetable oils, nuts, seeds, avocados, and fatty fish. Fatty fish, flax seeds, chia seeds, soybean, and walnuts are particularly high in omega-3s.

There have been numerous studies on diets that prioritize healthy unsaturated fats, in particular the Mediterranean diet, which receives recognition for being one of the healthiest diets in the world. This diet is rich in heart-healthy olive oil, fish, seafood, nuts, fruits, vegetables, and whole grains. This way of life also prioritizes social eating and community, which resonates with the second chakra.

Fats benefit the sacral chakra due to their indulgent and satiating nature. Many fats also have the ability to flow from a solid to a liquid state, embracing duality. Satisfying, sumptuous fats align with the svadhisthana, which is all about the richness in life. Additionally, many of these foods boost sexual health and wellness, which we will discuss further.

Fish, particularly salmon, is highly beneficial for balancing this chakra. Fish are composed of fluid essential fats and live in water, also resonating with the second chakra's element.

liquids and tropical fruits

With an element of water, it's only natural that liquid-based foods would support this chakra. It's important to stay well hydrated by drinking plenty of water and nutritious liquids. This can include coconut water, fruit-infused waters, teas, kombucha, juices (green and fruit), nut milks, smoothies, and more.

Liquid-based foods—such as bone broths, soups, and stews—and foods high in water content like cucumber and watermelon also balance this chakra. While many fruits have a high water content, tropical fruits in particular are known to resonate with the energy of the sacral chakra. Tropical fruits grow in warm, sunny climates and are very sweet and juicy, aligning with the "sweetness" and pleasure of the svadhisthana. These exotic fruits are depicted in art and history throughout different cultures for their sensual and aphrodisiac properties.

foods to support sexual health

I wrote a series of articles on foods for sexual health and function for *Healthline* a few years ago, and those articles account for at least 80 percent of the direct messages I receive. I get a lot of questions, which tells me that holistic sexual health is a concern and priority for many. And there's good news: From balancing sex hormones to improving blood flow, food helps support sexual and reproductive health in a variety of ways.

The second chakra is closely associated with the bladder, kidneys, and reproductive organs. When it comes to feeding this chakra, we can support it with foods that may boost sexual desire (aphrodisiacs), support overall sexual health, and assist in the healthy function of these associated organs.

Another way omega-3 fatty acids support the sacral chakra is by aiding in sexual and reproductive health. Omega-3s have been proven to help with circulation and blood flow, which may boost your libido, and have been shown to ease painful menstruation (especially when combined with vitamin E). Additionally, antioxidants can help improve overall blood flow and reduce oxidative stress, two key factors in libido and fertility. Foods high in antioxidants that benefit sexual health include pomegranates, apples, cranberries, and dark leafy greens.

We can also take note of foods proven to boost testosterone and estrogen production. Foods shown to increase estrogen levels include flax seeds, soy, fruit, and garlic, while foods like leafy greens, fatty fish, and avocados boost testosterone. Likewise, including more zinc in the diet may be helpful. Zinc helps the body with essential functions, such as stamina, regulating testosterone levels, and synthesizing thyroid hormones. Zinc has also been studied to improve libido and sexual function in postmenopausal women. Foods high in zinc include oysters, lobster, red meat, and pine nuts.

If you are looking to boost libido or sensuality to support the sacral chakra, consider trying aphrodisiacs. Studied aphrodisiacs consist of plants and herbs such as maca, ginkgo biloba, saffron, and fenugreek. Other popular foods—including chocolate, oysters, and chile peppers—have also been reported to exhibit aphrodisiac properties.

orange foods

As a proud member of the four-eyed club, I grew up being told to eat carrots for my eyesight, but never understood why. Orange foods like carrots are rich in beta-carotene, a pigmented compound present in plants known as carotenoids. Beta-carotene is an antioxidant that the body converts into fat-soluble vitamin A. Diets rich in carotenoids like beta-carotene support eye health, cognitive wellness, immune function, and more.

While orange foods deeply resonate with the vibration of this chakra, filling your plate with a variety of colors will also support the sacral. Try the "rainbow" recipes in this book to ignite creativity and inspire joy, such as Rainbow Summer Rolls (page 122), Rainbow Salad Jars (page 133), and Chakra Charcuterie (page 171).

list of sacral chakra foods

Healthy Fats & Omega-3-Rich Foods
Avocado
Chia seeds
Coconut
Edamame
Eggs
Flax seeds
Hemp seeds
Herring
Mackerel
Natto (fermented soybeans)
Olive oil
Olives
Oysters
Salmon
Sardines
Sea bass
Seaweed
Sesame oil
Shrimp
Tuna
Walnuts and other nuts

Liquids & Foods with High Water Content
Aloe vera juice
Apple
Broth and bone broth
Celery and celery juice
Coconut milk
Coconut water
Cucumber
Fruit-infused water
Green, vegetable, or fruit juice
Herbal tea
Kombucha
Nut milk
Smoothies
Soup
Water and sparkling water
Watermelon

Tropical Fruits
Açaí
Banana
Breadfruit
Coconut
Dragon fruit
Durian
Fig
Guava
Jackfruit
Kiwi
Lychee
Mamey sapote
Mango
Papaya
Passion fruit
Pineapple
Pomegranate
Pomelo
Prickly pear
Rambutan
Starfruit

Foods to Support Sexual Health
Apple
Avocado
Banana
Beet
Cacao and dark chocolate
Carrot
Chile pepper
Coffee
Cranberry
Eggs
Fenugreek
Garlic
Ginger
Ginkgo biloba
Ginseng
Grapes
Leafy greens
Maca
Nuts and seeds
Oats
Oysters
Pomegranate juice
Red wine
Saffron
Salmon
Spinach
Sweet potato
Tomato
Watermelon

Orange Foods
Apricot
Butternut squash
Cantaloupe
Carrot
Clementine
Egg yolk
Kabocha squash
Kumquat
Mamey sapote
Mango
Nectarine
Orange bell pepper
Orange
Orange tomato
Papaya
Peach
Persimmon
Pumpkin
Salmon
Salmon roe
Sweet potato
Tangerine

sacral chakra meal plan examples

	Breakfast	Lunch	Dinner	Snack
MONDAY	Tropical Bliss Smoothie (page 97)	Butternut Squash and Pear Soup (page 126)	Blueberry Balsamic Salmon (page 147)	Chakra Charcuterie (page 171)
TUESDAY	Peaches and Cream Chia Pudding (page 107)	Rainbow Salad Jars (page 133)	Miso Salmon Soba Noodle Bowls (page 138)	Chocolate-Dipped Stuffed Dates (page 175)
WEDNESDAY	Sacral Sweet Potato Toast (page 111)	Rainbow Summer Rolls (page 122)	Orange Sesame Tofu Stir-Fry (page 151)	Roasted Sweet Potato Hummus (page 169)
THURSDAY	Hawaiian Açaí Bowls (page 100)	Avocado toast on whole-grain or sprouted bread with lox, cucumber, capers, olive oil, and lemon	Sweet potato gnocchi with sautéed shrimp	Fresh tropical fruit salad with diced pineapple, kiwi, mango, dragon fruit, and watermelon
FRIDAY	Eggs fried in olive oil served with avocado slices, an orange, and a glass of carrot juice	Salad with tuna, orange bell peppers, edamame, sesame seeds, and Asian dressing	Carrot or pumpkin curry served with coconut rice	Seeded crackers and carrot sticks with olive tapenade

sacral chakra crystals

Use the following crystals to ignite passion, balance emotions, and inspire creativity to support the sacral chakra:

 aragonite This peach-colored cluster is sometimes called the "Stone of Truth." It promotes clarity, understanding, and personal growth. It is known for balancing negative emotions, especially anger and fear.

 carnelian Fiery carnelian has been one of the most popular fertility stones for centuries. This crystal is a popular choice for passion and creativity, making it a powerful sacral supporter.

 orange calcite This sunny stone is used for creativity and inspiration. It is said to alleviate lethargy and stagnation to make space for joy and self-expression. It has been used to support both sexual and digestive health.

 orange moonstone Associated with the lunar cycle and femininity, moonstone is typically used to harmonize women's physical energy. It is said to promote fertility, regulate mood, and cultivate compassion.

 sunstone Nurturing sunstone is believed to bring more "sweetness" to life— exactly what the svadhisthana represents. This sunset-hued stone encourages connection, vitality, creativity, and self-authenticity.

sacral chakra yoga poses

Practice the following yoga poses to help you unblock your second chakra and awaken your sensual and creative energies:

cat-cow (bitilasana-marjaryasana) Start on your hands and knees in a tabletop position with your wrists under your shoulders and your knees under your hips. Take a deep breath, allowing your back to gently curve as you lift your gaze toward the sky. As you exhale, arch your back, tuck your tailbone in, and shift your gaze toward your navel. Repeat this movement slowly and with intention.

goddess pose (utkata konasana) This squatting pose will relieve tight hip flexors, encourage flexibility in the pelvis and spine, and strengthen your lower body. Start by positioning yourself in a wide stance with your feet facing outward at a 90-degree angle. Bend your knees until your thighs are parallel to the floor while maintaining a straight spine. Bring your hands together in front of your heart center and take deep breaths while sinking into this pose.

low lunge (anjaneyasana) Begin in a tabletop position, aligning your wrists beneath your shoulders and your knees beneath your hips. From there, bring your left foot forward and between your hands, ensuring the foot is flat on the ground and pointing straight. Bring your hands to your thigh or raise your arms above your head and sink your hips toward the floor as you lengthen your spine and feel this full stretch. Switch legs and repeat.

reclined bound angle pose (supta baddha konasana) Improve blood flow to the pelvis and release tension with this relaxing hip opener that's ideal for all levels. Enter this pose by lying on your back. Open your legs wide until they are in a diamond shape and the soles of your feet touch, allowing your knees to naturally fall open to the sides. Place your palms on your belly. Remain in this pose for several minutes, allowing gravity to open and stretch your groin and hip area.

reverse warrior pose (viparita virabhadrasana) Enter this posture by standing at the top of your mat. Step one foot back (about 4 feet, or 1 m), turning it to a 45-degree angle while keeping your front foot facing forward. Bend your front knee directly over your ankle and stretch your arms out to a "T" shape at shoulder height. Looking up at the ceiling, gently reach the front arm upward as you lean your upper body back. Hold for five breaths and repeat on the opposite side.

sacral chakra affirmations

I can create and live a life of joy.

My life is mine to design and manifest.

I open myself up for creativity and passion to flow through me.

I deserve pleasure in my life.

I give myself permission to create, explore, and play.

I embrace my inner child, nurturing my creativity to blossom.

I let go of any guilt or shame I may have about my emotions and desires.

I fully embrace and celebrate my sexuality.

I am a lovable and desirable being.

I am in touch with my feelings and emotions.

It is safe for me to express myself freely and speak my truth.

I am grateful for everything my body does for me.

I listen to my body's needs and nourish it with healthful foods.

It's safe to get close to people.

I accept change and the natural flow of life.

more ways to support the sacral chakra

emotional catharsis Emotional catharsis can be a healthy way to connect with your raw emotions and express them. This can be done by certain exercises (such as kickboxing, dance, jumping, etc.), progressive muscle relaxation, psychodrama therapy, and more.

journal Journaling can also be a form of emotional catharsis and something that many find a beneficial habit.

practice self-care and body positivity Practice loving and embracing your body and all that it does for you. Read body positivity books or follow similar social channels, get a massage, or make daily body gratitude exercises a habit.

see a sex therapist Qualified sex therapists can help address everything from past sexual trauma to lack of desire. If you need more support with intimacy issues, this is a great option.

spend time in water Connect with the second chakra's element of water and spend time at the beach, swimming, or doing your favorite water activities. If you don't live near bodies of water, take a relaxing herbal salt bath.

try a new creative outlet Find a new hobby that you enjoy (think: watercolor painting, photography, or jewelry making). Free or low-cost options can easily be found at hobby shops, local events, and even online. Remember that you don't have to be "great" to enjoy a hobby or creative outlet. The joy is in the process, not in the result.

solar plexus chakra

sanskrit name
MANIPURA

element
FIRE

location
LOWER ABDOMEN
(BETWEEN THE NAVEL
AND RIB CAGE)

characteristics
POWER, ENERGY,
CONFIDENCE,
VITALITY, SELF-
WORTH, EGO, IDENTITY,
TRANSFORMATION

color
YELLOW

Our third chakra is the solar plexus, or *manipura* in Sanskrit. *Mani* means "jewel" or "gem," while *pura* means "place" or "city." Therefore, this chakra translates into "city of jewels." This conveys that the solar plexus is a central hub for the body's vitality, power, and self-worth.

The third chakra is all about our personal power and identity. This includes our confidence, willpower, self-esteem, and the resilience to transform and grow. Individuals who possess a well-balanced solar plexus believe in themselves, radiate confidence, and demonstrate willpower and determination.

On the contrary, an unbalanced solar plexus chakra will manifest in low self-esteem, lack of confidence, low energy, or a loss of identity. An overactive third chakra may translate into aggression, perfectionism, and extreme arrogant or dominating personality traits.

Fire, the element of this chakra, symbolizes both vitality and transformation. Fire has the capacity to transform one element into another, such as converting fuel into light, power, or heat. As I was writing this chapter, I began to think of the phrase "fire in your belly" and how much it relates to this chakra. If you have a "fire" in your belly, it means that you are enthusiastic, confident, and energetic—all of the trademarks of the solar plexus. Even more, this is where the solar plexus is located, governing our digestive health and metabolism.

Since the location of our third chakra is in the stomach area, it's not surprising that food holds significance here. Food fuels this chakra in a multitude of ways, including "firing" up the digestive system and converting itself into pure energy. Food also possesses the power to transform us.

Let's regain power over our energy levels and overall vitality as we feed our third chakra.

feeding your solar plexus chakra

To feed our solar plexus, we concentrate on complex carbohydrates, whole grains, and warming foods. We can also balance the third chakra with foods that are yellow, resonating with the color of the manipura, and foods that support digestive health.

whole grains and complex carbohydrates

Carbohydrates are broken into two groups: simple and complex. Simple carbohydrates are quickly digested and turned into energy, but lead to rapid spikes in blood sugar levels. Examples of foods high in simple carbs include sugar, candy, baked goods, processed foods, soda, and certain high-sugar fruits.

Complex carbohydrates, on the other hand, take a longer time for the body to digest and provide more continuous levels of energy. Whole grains, legumes, starchy vegetables, fruits, nuts, and seeds are some examples of complex carbs. These foods are rich in fiber, vitamins, and minerals.

Not all simple carbohydrates are "unhealthy," especially when in the form of whole fruits or when consumed in limited moderation. However, when it comes to fueling the body and the solar plexus, complex carbohydrates are an obvious choice due to the nutrients and sustained energy they provide. Additionally, complex carbs and whole grains have been proven to reduce the risk of several chronic health conditions, including cardiovascular disease and type 2 diabetes.

When it comes to whole grains, it's easy to make a few swaps or incorporate more into your daily diet. One simple way is by replacing white pastas, breads, or cereals with 100 percent whole grain or whole wheat varieties. You can also make whole-grain recipes yourself, starting your morning with homemade granola (Cranberry Chai Granola, page 113), layering fiber-full grain bowls (Build-Your-Own Savory Breakfast Bowls, page 114), or adding heart-healthy grains to salads (Amethyst Barley and Lentil Salad, page 118). These whole grains and complex carbs will energize and fuel both the body and the third chakra.

spicy and warming foods

Take note of the third chakra's fire element and add heat to your diet. Heat can be obtained from both spicy and "warming" foods. Warming foods have the ability to increase body temperature and boost metabolism through their thermogenic effect.

In Ayurveda, foods are classified as either heating or calming, depending on their energetic properties and impact on the body's dosha types. Having a balance of these foods is important to the solar plexus. Warming foods include whole grains, root vegetables, hot beverages, and spices such as ginger, black pepper, cinnamon, turmeric, cloves, nutmeg, and mustard. When it comes to spicy foods, it's no sweat to add a little fire: Cook with or complement meals with chile peppers, red pepper flakes, hot sauces, harissa, wasabi, and more.

foods to support digestive health

Since the third chakra is closely associated with the stomach, liver, gallbladder, pancreas, and small intestines, we can feed the solar plexus with foods to support these organs, which make up our digestive system. A healthy digestive system is essential for breaking down food into nutrients, which the body uses for energy and cell repair.

Fiber-rich foods such as whole grains, fruits, vegetables, legumes, and nuts support digestive health. Additionally, probiotics play a crucial role in gut health. Probiotics are "good" bacteria that live in your digestive tract. Foods and fermented products, including yogurt, kefir, sauerkraut, kimchi, and kombucha, contain these live microorganisms.

Probiotics support a balanced gut microbiome, boost immune health, and have even been shown to improve mood and some mental health disorders. This is due to the communication network between the gastrointestinal tract and the central nervous system, also known as the "gut-brain axis."

yellow foods

Since the solar plexus vibrates at the same frequency as the color yellow, foods such as corn, lemons, saffron, pineapples, bananas, and mangoes balance this chakra. These foods receive their golden hue from carotenoid pigments like lutein and beta-carotene.

Yellow foods share many of the same traits as orange foods when it comes to supporting eye, immune, and skin health. In addition, yellow foods are especially beneficial for your gastrointestinal tract and the gut microbiome. These foods—particularly yellow onions, bananas, whole grains, legumes, potatoes, and oats—are rich in prebiotic fiber, which supports overall digestive health.

list of solar plexus chakra foods

Whole Grains & Legumes

Amaranth
Barley
Beans
Brown rice
Buckwheat
Bulgur
Farro
Freekeh
Lentils
Lupini
Millet
Oats
Peanuts
Peas
Quinoa
Spelt
Whole wheat

Other Complex Carbs

Apple
Artichoke
Beet
Carrot
Dates
Fig
Grapes
Kiwi
Mango
Parsnip
Pear
Pineapple
Plantain
Potato
Pumpkin
Raisins
Root vegetables
Squash
Sweet potato

Spicy & Warming Foods

Anise
Black pepper
Cacao and dark chocolate
Chile pepper
Cinnamon
Clove
Coriander
Cumin
Fennel
Garlic
Ginger
Ginseng
Gochujang
Harissa
Horseradish
Nutmeg
Onion
Peppercorn
Root vegetables
Rosemary
Turmeric
Vinegar
Wasabi
Whole-grain mustard
Whole grains

Foods to Support Digestive Health

Bone broth
Chia seeds
Fennel
Ginger
Kefir
Kimchi
Kombucha
Leafy greens
Lentils
Miso

Natto (fermented soybean)
Papaya
Pear
Peppermint
Sauerkraut
Tempeh
Whole grains
Yogurt

Yellow Foods

Asian pear
Banana
Cheese
Corn
Durian
Ghee
Honey
Jackfruit
Lemon
Mango
Mustard
Parsnip
Passion fruit
Pattypan squash
Pear
Pineapple
Quince
Saffron
Starfruit
Turmeric
Yellow apple
Yellow beet
Yellow bell pepper
Yellow carrot
Yellow cauliflower
Yellow onion
Yellow potato
Yellow tomato
Yellow wax beans
Zucchini flowers

solar plexus chakra meal plan examples

	Breakfast	Lunch	Dinner	Snack
MONDAY	Build-Your-Own Savory Breakfast Bowls (page 114)	Butternut Squash and Pear Soup (page 126)	Miso Salmon Soba Noodle Bowls (page 138)	Turmeric Tea Three Ways (page 84)
TUESDAY	Tropical Coconut Chia Pudding (page 107)	Crispy Cauliflower Pitas with Turmeric Tahini (page 136)	Shrimp Tacos with Grilled Corn and Pineapple Salsa (page 142)	Grilled Corn and Pineapple Salsa (page 142) served with tortilla chips or yellow bell pepper strips
WEDNESDAY	Cinnamon Apple Quinoa Porridge (page 110)	Amethyst Barley and Lentil Salad (page 118)	Soul-Warming Kitchari (page 161)	Vanilla yogurt topped with sliced bananas and cinnamon
THURSDAY	Greek yogurt with sliced apple, pear, or banana and Cranberry Chai Granola (page 113)	Sandwich on whole wheat bread served with carrot sticks and lemon hummus	Turkey Picadillo Stuffed Peppers (page 156)	Rice cakes topped with peanut butter and raisins
FRIDAY	Whole wheat toast with peanut butter, sliced banana, and chopped peanuts	Spicy yellow curry or lentil soup	Spaghetti squash with spicy tomato sauce	Mango sorbet or sliced fresh mango and a glass of kombucha

solar plexus chakra crystals

Use the following crystals to restore emotional balance, confidence, and energy to support your third chakra:

 agate Supporting transformation, vitality, and growth, agate is a versatile and warm stone that radiates cleansing volcanic energy. Yellow agate balances the solar plexus chakra by regulating negative emotions and encouraging confidence, prosperity, and courage.

 citrine Golden citrine, associated with abundance and positivity, provides warm and pure healing energy. This crystal can be used to increase confidence, motivation, and personal power. Like many other yellow crystals, citrine is linked with supporting healthy digestion and metabolism.

 pyrite Often referred to as "Fool's Gold," this gleaming golden nugget is said to manifest success, wealth, and vitality. Taking its name from the ancient Greek word for "fire," pyrite can help encourage confidence and overcome fears.

 tiger's eye Reclaim self-confidence and fearlessness, deflect negative energy from others, and obtain protection with this radiant striped stone. Tiger's eye, a supporter of all three lower chakras, helps you activate your personal power and ignite your inner fire.

 yellow topaz The word topaz comes from the Sanskrit word *tapas*, which means "heat" or "fire." Golden topaz is a powerful stone for supporting vitality, a sense of empowerment, and mental clarity.

solar plexus chakra yoga poses

Practice the following yoga poses to find vitality and strength while helping to unblock your solar plexus chakra:

boat pose (navasana) Stimulate the abdominal organs, improve digestion, and activate core strength with boat pose. Enter this pose by sitting with your legs out in front of you. Simultaneously and slowly, lift your legs and lean back to balance on your sit bones and create a "V" shape. Breathe deeply and calmly while keeping your spine straight and engaging your core.

bow pose (dhanurasana) Another helpful pose to aid in digestion, bow pose can stretch and strengthen back muscles while balancing the solar plexus. To practice this pose, start by lying on your stomach. Bend your knees and reach back to grab your ankles. As you inhale, lift your chest and thighs off the ground, creating a bow-like shape with your body.

reverse plank pose (purvottanasana) Plank poses are arm-balancing stretches that open your chest and fire up your abdomen and core. To do a reverse plank, begin in a seated position with your legs extended in front of you. Place your hands behind you and point your fingers toward your toes. Slowly push your hips off the ground and create a straight line from your head to your heels. Breathe as you engage your core and press firmly through your palms.

sun mudra (surya mudra) Mudras are simple hand gestures used in yoga and meditation. This mudra activates the body's inner fire element, encouraging energy and transformation. To perform sun mudra, sit in a comfortable position with your legs crossed. Place the tip of your ring fingers against the inner base of your thumbs. Create gentle pressure with your thumbs and keep the other fingers extended. Breathe calmly and deeply.

warrior ii pose (virabhadrasana ii) Unlock your personal power with warrior poses. To perform Warrior II pose, enter this posture by standing at the top of your mat. Step one foot back (about 3 feet, or 1 m), turning it to a 45-degree angle while keeping your front foot facing forward. Bend your front knee directly over your ankle and stretch your arms out to a "T" shape at shoulder height. Hold this pose for a few calming breaths and repeat on the opposite side.

solar plexus affirmations

I embrace my personal power.

I am strong and capable.

I let go of limiting beliefs and choose to trust myself.

I release all of my fears and doubts and embrace what's next.

I am driven to fulfill my purpose.

I have complete confidence in my abilities and the value I bring.

I am capable of accomplishing anything I set my mind to.

I am fearless in the pursuit of what sets my soul on fire.

I am determined and fully receptive to achieving success.

I am worthy of success and abundance.

I am allowed to take up space.

I choose to prioritize myself.

I am filled with energy and vitality.

I do not let others define my self-worth.

I am worthy of respect from myself and others.

more ways to support the solar plexus chakra

essential oils Warming and woodsy essential oils such as black pepper, cedarwood, ginger, rosemary, and lemongrass balance the third chakra.

say "hello" to heat Channel the fire element and warm things up by embracing heat. From taking a hot yoga class to sitting by a bonfire while camping to sunbathing (with sunscreen!), do this however feels best for you.

try something new The solar plexus chakra is all about courage and embracing your personal power. What better way to do that than to step outside your comfort zone and try something new?

boost your energy Although we talked about the importance of food when it comes to energy, there are many other ways to improve your energy and vitality. While exercise and proper amounts of sleep are vital, research also shows that reducing and controlling stress enhances overall energy levels. Incorporate stress management into your daily routine by practicing relaxation techniques such as breathing exercises, meditation, yoga, and mindfulness.

embrace a growth mindset Consistently learning and challenging yourself will not only build confidence, but also add to your current skills and abilities. Cultivate a growth mindset by setting goals, learning from failures and mistakes, and embracing challenges.

heart chakra

sanskrit name
ANAHATA

location
CENTER OF THE CHEST

color
GREEN

element
AIR

characteristics
LOVE, COMPASSION,
CONNECTION, EMPATHY,
GENEROSITY, FORGIVENESS,
AND HARMONY

The fourth chakra is certainly the easiest to define simply by its name. The heart chakra is all about love, compassion, and connection. The Sanskrit name for the fourth chakra, *anahata*, means "unstruck" or "unhurt." This symbolizes the boundless love, purity, and compassion of the heart chakra. Additionally, anahata refers to the Vedic concept of the "unstruck" sound, an eternal and divine sound that is created without physical means.

Located in the center of the chest, the heart chakra is the bridge between the lower three and upper three chakras. Here, we begin to move from the physical realm of the first three chakras into the higher consciousness of the upper chakras. This becomes clear as we shift our focus to the fourth chakra's element, air, and transcend beyond the realm of tangible physical elements. Air is symbolic to this chakra for many reasons. Free-flowing and unrestricted, air is a vital life force that is associated with openness, harmony, and unity. We all breathe the same air.

The heart chakra consists of love in all forms: self-love, love for others, and unconditional and divine love. It is the epitome of kindness, compassion, forgiveness, and acceptance. Individuals with a balanced heart chakra are able to have harmonious and healthy relationships, exhibit empathy, and give and receive love easily. They approach and live their lives with an open heart, feel inner peace, and are capable of forgiving themselves and others.

A blocked heart chakra can manifest in various emotional and physical ways. An imbalanced fourth chakra can make it difficult to express or receive love, resulting in feelings of loneliness, isolation, or fear of rejection. A blocked heart chakra can look like being in toxic relationships, being unable to forgive oneself or others, and unresolved grief, trauma, or heartache. Physical symptoms associated with this chakra include respiratory issues, chest discomfort, and poor circulation. However, it is extremely important to always consult a healthcare professional to address any physical concerns.

Since the fourth chakra represents harmony, a heart chakra–supporting diet will place emphasis on balance. The heart chakra recipes in this book feature a balance of macros (protein, carbohydrates, and fats) in addition to the foods in the following section. To further open the heart and feed this chakra, cook for or with someone you love. Cooking in itself can harmonize the anahata. If you have ever heard that a dish was "made with love," it means the person cooking it opened their heart chakra to cook with intention, care, and gratitude. Cooking and sharing meals with others is a very meaningful way to connect.

feeding your heart chakra

To harmonize our heart chakra, we concentrate on incorporating cruciferous vegetables, leafy greens, and other green foods into our diet. We also focus on these nourishing foods and others to help promote optimal heart health.

cruciferous vegetables

The vast majority of cruciferous vegetables are rich in vibrant green pigments that resonate with the heart chakra's energy. These fiber-rich vegetables support heart health while aiding in the body's detoxification process thanks to the bioactive compounds they contain. Detoxing supports the heart chakra's ability to heal from negative emotions and release what no longer serves us. Examples of cruciferous vegetables include broccoli, cauliflower, arugula, kale, cabbage, and brussels sprouts.

leafy greens

Many leafy greens fall into all of the heart chakra food categories here. Deemed "superfoods" for good reason, leafy greens are rich sources of vitamins, minerals, and antioxidants that help remove toxins from the body. Additionally, leafy greens are typically eaten raw, and raw foods are believed to contain a higher amount of *prana* (life force energy). Many believe that consuming raw foods may help the body better process and release "big" emotions. As far as what science has to say on that subject, there is clear evidence that links raw fruits and vegetables to better overall mental health and mood.

foods to support heart health

An open heart starts with a healthy heart, and what we eat is the most important factor in heart health. Eating healthy fats, whole grains, lean proteins, and a rainbowed medley of fruits and vegetables is the key to cardiovascular health and vitality. The American Heart Association studied fruits and vegetables associated with improved cardiovascular health and noted that leafy greens, pome fruits (e.g., apples), citrus fruits, cruciferous vegetables, carrots, and alliums (e.g., garlic) have the most significant benefits of all produce.

green foods

Green foods resonate harmoniously with the heart chakra, aligning with its verdant energy of growth, balance, interconnectedness, and compassion.

Green foods derive their color from the plant pigment chlorophyll. During photosynthesis, plants use chlorophyll to absorb the sun's radiant energy and fuel a complex biochemical reaction that produces essential nutrients. Like the heart, chlorophyll provides and sustains life, vitality, and energy. Chlorophyll-rich foods not only supply a vibrant green color, but they also offer vitamins, minerals, antioxidants, and other beneficial compounds that support overall health and well-being. Besides chlorophyll, green foods are rich in a variety of micronutrients and phytochemicals that promote healthy blood flow and support the cardiovascular system.

Pink can also resonate with this love-centered chakra, so eating pink foods (like Pink Pitaya Coconut Truffles, page 164) may help open the heart.

list of heart chakra foods

Cruciferous Vegetables
Arugula
Bok choy
Broccoli
Broccoli rabe
Brussels sprouts
Cabbage
Cauliflower
Chard
Collard greens
Horseradish
Kale
Kohlrabi
Radish
Rutabaga
Turnip
Wasabi
Watercress

Leafy Greens & Herbs
Arugula
Basil
Bay leaf
Beet greens
Bibb lettuce
Chervil
Chive
Cilantro
Collard greens
Dandelion greens
Dill
Iceberg lettuce
Kale
Marjoram
Mint
Mustard greens
Oregano
Parsley

Rapini
Romaine lettuce
Rosemary
Sage
Savory
Sorrel
Spinach
Swiss chard
Tarragon
Thyme
Turnip greens
Watercress

Foods to Support Heart Health
Apple
Avocado
Beans
Berries
Cherries
Citrus fruits
Dark chocolate
Edamame
Fatty fish
Fish oil
Garlic
Grapes
Green tea
Herbs
Leafy greens
Legumes
Nuts and seeds
Oatmeal
Olive oil
Pomegranate
Red wine
Sweet potato
Swiss chard

Tofu
Tomato
Whole grains
Yogurt

Other Green Foods
Alfalfa sprouts
Artichoke
Asparagus
Bitter melon
Celery
Chayote
Cucumber
Fennel
Gooseberries
Green beans
Green lentils
Green pepper
Green pumpkin
Honeydew
Kiwi
Leek
Lemongrass
Lima beans
Lime
Matcha
Microgreens
Mung beans
Nopal
Okra
Pear
Peas
Romanesco
Seaweed
Snow peas
Spring onion
Sugar snap peas
Zucchini

heart chakra meal plan examples

	Breakfast	Lunch	Dinner	Snack
MONDAY	Green Glow Juice (page 93)	Chopped Greek Kale Salad (page 128)	Green Goddess Buddha Bowls (page 144)	Matcha Frozen Yogurt Bark (page 167)
TUESDAY	Matcha Raspberry Chia Pudding (page 106)	Dandelion Greens Salad with Strawberries and Goat Cheese (page 125)	Kale Pesto Pasta with Spring Vegetables (page 148)	Pink Pitaya Coconut Truffles (page 164)
WEDNESDAY	Green smoothie served with an apple	Rainbow Salad Jars (page 133)	Mediterranean Mezze Bowls with Quinoa (page 152)	Summer Fruit Salad with Ginger-Lime Dressing (page 176)
THURSDAY	Green shakshuka or a spinach-herb omelet	Roasted Purple Cauliflower Soup (page 130)	Lemon and herb chicken served with whole wheat couscous and sautéed garlic kale	Green grapes or nut butter–stuffed celery served with iced green tea
FRIDAY	Oatmeal or overnight oats with fresh berries and nuts	Chicken and broccoli served with brown rice	Grilled or sautéed fish served with brussels sprouts and cauliflower rice	Baked kale chips with lemon hummus

heart chakra crystals

Use the following crystals to inspire love, cultivate compassion, and clear heart chakra blockages:

emerald A stone of compassion and prosperity, emerald teaches us to trust our intuition and our own heart while finding harmony with ourselves and others. This gorgeously green gem is said to strengthen relationships by fostering deeper connections, loyalty, and understanding.

green aventurine Enhance empathy, promote emotional balance, and heal heart chakra blockages with glistening green aventurine. This crystal, referred to as the "Stone of Opportunity," can also attract abundance, prosperity, and good luck.

jade This healing gem is known for its ability to nurture positive energy, attract romantic love, and encourage prosperity and abundance. Green jade stimulates the heart space and is considered a symbol of vitality and longevity in certain cultures.

rhodonite This stunning speckled pink stone takes its name from the ancient Greek word for "rose." Rich with heart-healing properties, rhodonite can help release past trauma, break unhealthy patterns, and cultivate forgiveness.

rose quartz Commonly known as the "Love Stone," this powerful pink crystal imbues a soothing, calming energy and helps open the heart to give and receive love. Rose quartz encourages empathy, self-love, compassion, forgiveness, and emotional healing.

heart chakra yoga poses

Practice the following chest-opening yoga poses to activate and balance the heart chakra:

cow pose (bitilasana) Expand the heart center and foster a sense of openness and compassion with cow pose. To enter this pose, start in a tabletop position on all fours. Inhale while you lower the belly, lift your chest, and point your tailbone up. This will create a gentle curve in your spine and open the chest.

dancer's pose (natarajasana) Align with the heart chakra's energetic qualities by performing this graceful chest-opener. To enter this pose, stand on one leg while you bend the opposite knee to lift the foot behind you. Hold your lifted foot or ankle with the hand on the same side. Extend your other arm while you lean forward and lift your chest, creating a gentle backbend and finding your balance.

locust pose (salabhasana) Strengthen your legs and core, open your chest, and stretch your lower back while harmonizing your heart chakra. To enter this pose, start by lying flat on your belly. Lift your chest and legs off the ground simultaneously while keeping your arms by your sides and gazing at the floor in front of you. Hold for a few breaths, then slowly release.

upward facing dog (urdhva mukha svanasana) Open your heart and strengthen the upper body with this powerful backbend. Begin by lying on your stomach with the tops of your feet flat on the floor. Bend your elbows, placing your hands on the floor next to your rib cage, and spread your fingers wide. Pressing through the palms of your hands and the tops of your feet, lift your chest and upper body off the ground while keeping your legs extended behind you. Press your elbows tightly against your sides and direct your gaze toward the sky as you open your heart.

wheel pose (chakrasana) This advanced deep backbend opens the heart and entire front body. Lie on your back to enter this pose. Place your hands under your shoulders with your fingers pointing in the direction of your feet. Press into your hands and feet as you lift your hips and chest off the ground, creating an arch while keeping your knees hip-width apart. The body needs to be fully warmed up before attempting this pose.

heart chakra affirmations

My heart is open.

I am open to give and receive love.

I love and accept myself unconditionally.

I deserve to experience genuine and unwavering love.

I lovingly nurture my mind, body, and spirit.

I lead my life with gratitude and compassion.

I am open to give and receive kindness.

I can find light within the darkness. If I cannot find it, I can be it.

I am attracting trusting and loving relationships.

I am worthy of self-care.

My happiness comes from within me.

I give myself permission to feel pure happiness and joy.

I release feelings of resentment and choose forgiveness in order to find inner peace.

I am never alone.

I forgive myself for my mistakes and I grow from them.

I choose compassion and release judgment.

I am united with all beings.

I am allowed to heal.

more ways to support the heart chakra

essential oils Soothing scents like rose, jasmine, bergamot, lavender, and geranium can help balance and open the fourth chakra.

volunteer Volunteering can open the heart chakra as you cultivate compassion, empathy, and generosity. Volunteer with a local nonprofit or help cook a meal for those in need.

start a gratitude journal Begin journaling three things you are grateful for (and why) each day. Studies have shown that practicing gratitude can help with lowered stress, better sleep, and improved interpersonal relationships.

make time for self-care We know the benefits of self-care when it comes to promoting overall well-being and opening the fourth chakra. Now it's time to practice it. Not limited to just spa days, self-care can be whatever makes you personally feel nurtured and cared for.

foster meaningful connections The heart chakra encourages deep connections and fulfilling relationships. To balance this chakra, spend time with loved ones and nurture your current relationships or open yourself up to new ones. If you are struggling with loneliness, join a club or social group to create new connections.

throat chakra

sanskrit name
VISHUDDHA

location
THROAT REGION

color
BLUE

element
ETHER

characteristics
COMMUNICATION,
SELF-EXPRESSION,
AUTHENTICITY, TRUTH,
CLARITY, LISTENING

The throat chakra, also known as *vishuddha* in Sanskrit, is the fifth chakra. Meaning "pure," the vishuddha governs our expression, communication, and authenticity. Located in the throat region, the fifth chakra is also closely connected to the thyroid gland, mouth, tongue, palate, nose, and ears.

The throat chakra's element is ether, which is the upper regions of space or the heavens. Ether symbolizes the vastness of human expression and the ability to move beyond ourselves to find higher truth. This is the beginning of the upper three chakras, which all represent higher states of consciousness and the journey toward spiritual enlightenment.

Our throat functions as a pathway for both breath and sound. The throat chakra serves as a channel through which our inner truths and ideas can be vocalized and communicated to the outside world. Authentic self-expression, effective communication, and the capacity to listen and understand are the defining characteristics of a well-balanced throat chakra. Individuals with a centered fifth chakra will convey their thoughts and emotions openly and honestly, contribute creatively, and listen attentively when others speak.

On the other hand, a blocked or imbalanced throat chakra can lead to challenges in communication and authentic self-expression. Difficulties in speaking one's truth, fear of judgment, or feeling silenced can arise. Physical symptoms are said to include thyroid issues, throat soreness, and tension in the neck and shoulders.

Food is naturally important to a chakra that is located within the mouth, tongue, palate, and nose. When balancing this chakra, we can think beyond substance and draw our attention to the smells, tastes, and textures of our food. We can actively engage all of our senses and concentrate on the various flavors we are experiencing—salty, sweet, spicy, sour, or bitter. This is mindful eating.

Besides the foods in the following section, cooking itself can balance the throat chakra. Cooking can be an act of self-expression, artistry, self-discovery, and authenticity. I think of this especially when someone learns or cooks food from their heritage or culture. I also think of chefs I know who have difficulty verbally communicating but express themselves and their truth beautifully through their food. I believe that cooking can be a powerful conduit to help heal or balance the fifth chakra.

feeding your throat chakra

To balance the throat chakra, we can feed it with soothing foods, blue foods, sea vegetables, and foods to support thyroid health and function.

soothing and hydrating foods

Calming, hydrating foods support the fifth chakra and throat. These foods can include what you would eat if you had a sore throat—think: herbal teas, soups, smoothies, water-dense fruits, warm oatmeal, or yogurt. Honey and herbs such as chamomile, mint, and lavender also have a strong soothing effect on the throat. Throat-healing honey, known for its medicinal properties and antibacterial activity, can symbolize the sweetness of self-authenticity.

sea vegetables

Sea vegetables are edible plants, seaweed, or algae that come from oceans, seas, and other bodies of salt water. Common sea plants include nori, kelp, wakame, and spirulina. Rich in vitamins and minerals, sea plants have a variety of benefits, containing an abundance of antioxidants and supporting gut health with its prebiotic fiber. Many Asian countries have eaten diets rich in sea plants for centuries. On a recent trip to Kyoto, Japan, I enjoyed hearing stories from our *ryokan* owner about how she and other women ate a lot of seaweed when they were young to ensure beautiful, long hair while she served us miso soup, nori-wrapped rice, and kombu *tsukudani*.

Seaweed's iodine content makes it highly beneficial for thyroid health. The body requires iodine to produce thyroid hormones, and because it cannot generate iodine on its own, it must be obtained through food. Seaweed is considered one of the best natural sources of this essential mineral. It is worth noting that while iodine is crucial for health, excessive consumption of it can also contribute to or exacerbate thyroid problems. Ensuring a balanced intake of iodine through a diverse diet is essential for promoting health and proper thyroid function.

foods to support thyroid health

While seaweed tops the list, there are several other foods that can support overall thyroid health. These foods include seafood, fish, eggs, Brazil nuts, dairy, dark chocolate, and more. Besides iodine, foods that are rich in selenium, zinc, omega-3 fatty acids, vitamin D, and iron play a significant role in thyroid function.

blue foods

Unlike green, yellow, or red, blue plant pigments are very uncommon. This is because the blue pigments that are found in foods, such as anthocyanins, change color depending on the pH levels of the environment. We see this in real time with butterfly pea flowers (Butterfly Pea Tea Color-Changing Cooler, page 91), which change from blue to purple when an acid is introduced. Although rare to find a "true" blue food, blue-toned foods still contain anthocyanins that possess powerful anticancer and anti-inflammatory effects. These antioxidants have been shown to help prevent cardiovascular disease and boost brain health, which we will delve deeper into in the third eye section.

list of throat chakra foods

Soothing & Hydrating Foods

Aloe vera
Apple
Berries
Cantaloupe
Celery
Coconut water
Cucumber
Grapefruit
Herbal tea
Honey
Juices
Oatmeal
Peach
Smoothies
Soup
Watermelon
Yogurt
Zucchini

Sea Vegetables

Agar-agar
Aonori
Arame
Badderlocks
Dulse
Hijiki
Irish moss
Kelp
Kombu
Nori
Oarweed
Ogonori
Salicornia
Sea lettuce
Spirulina
Umibudo
Wakame

Foods to Support Thyroid Health

Apple
Avocado
Beans
Beef
Berries
Brazil nuts
Broccoli
Chicken
Citrus fruits
Cruciferous vegetables
Dark chocolate
Eggs
Fish
Green tea
Legumes
Milk
Nuts
Pear
Seaweed
Seeds
Shellfish
Whole grains
Yogurt

Blue Foods

Adirondack blue potato
Blackberries
Black currants
Blueberries
Blue corn
Blue crab
Blue spirulina
Blue tomato
Butterfly pea flowers
Concord grapes
Damson plum
Elderberries

throat chakra meal plan examples

	Breakfast	Lunch	Dinner	Snack
MONDAY	Blueberry Kale Smoothie (page 88)	Cucumber Seaweed Salad (page 129)	Blueberry Balsamic Salmon (page 147) served with brown rice and green beans	Butterfly Pea Tea Color-Changing Cooler (page 91)
TUESDAY	Blueberry Almond Chia Pudding (page 104)	Rainbow Summer Rolls (page 122)	Soul-Warming Kitchari (page 161)	Summer Fruit Salad with Ginger-Lime Dressing (page 176)
WEDNESDAY	Blue Spirulina Superfood Smoothie Bowl (page 103)	Roasted Purple Cauliflower Soup (page 130)	Turkey Picadillo Stuffed Peppers (page 156)	Salted Honey and Maca Fudge (page 172)
THURSDAY	Grapefruit or cantaloupe with cottage cheese and honey, served with herbal tea	Chicken with roasted sesame broccoli	Salmon and avocado sushi rolls	Brazil nut trail mix
FRIDAY	Scrambled eggs served with sliced avocado and fresh berries	Miso soup	Whole-grain bowls with protein of choice and lemon yogurt sauce	Fresh blueberries served with cold coconut water

throat chakra crystals

Use the following crystals to inspire self-expression and open space for truth and communication to support the throat chakra:

 amazonite Find harmony and balance with this calming crystal. Amazonite is strongly associated with both the heart and throat chakras, and can promote self-confidence, open expression, and emotional healing.

 aquamarine Stay connected to your true voice and express yourself without fear by keeping this soothing blue-green stone nearby. Associated with water, the aquamarine crystal helps you communicate with ease and fluidity.

 blue lace agate Find solace in expressing your authentic self to the world while cultivating a sense of composure and confidence with blue lace agate. This tranquil crystal allows us to access our highest truths and share our hopes, concerns, and dreams effortlessly.

 lapis lazuli This striking blue and gold-speckled stone inspires truth, open communication, and inner wisdom. Lapis lazuli, believed to boost confidence and clarity in communication, is a helpful stone for public speaking.

 turquoise This vibrant blue-green stone can help you express your thoughts and feelings with confidence and clarity. In addition to self-expression and empowerment, turquoise is believed beneficial in healing and releasing emotional blockages.

throat chakra yoga poses

Practice the following yoga poses to engage the upper body, open the throat, and balance the vishuddha chakra:

camel pose (ustrasana) Lengthen your throat and chest with this deep backbend. To perform camel pose, kneel on your mat, engage your core, and arch your back while keeping your hips aligned above your knees. Reach for your heels (or lower back) as you create a backbend, feeling a stretch in your throat and chest.

fish pose (matsyasana) Open your neck and establish a deeper connection with your breath as you welcome strength and self-expression. To enter fish pose, begin by lying on your back. Then, raise your chest, arch your back, and allow the top of your head to rest on the floor. Maintain an open and relaxed throat and neck as you breathe.

lion's breath (simha pranayama) This pranayama (breathing exercise) resembles a lion's roar and stimulates the throat chakra while releasing tension. To do this exercise, sit in a comfortable position. Open your mouth wide, stick your tongue out, and exhale forcefully while making an audible "ha" sound. As you exhale, stretch your face muscles by opening your eyes and eyebrows widely.

shoulder stand (sarvangasana) Inversions like shoulder stand promote blood flow to the throat and neck, which supports the fifth chakra. To practice this pose, lie on your back and lift your legs and hips straight up vertically while supporting your lower back with your hands. You can use folded blankets under the shoulders for additional support.

simple neck stretches If you're not able to do or are not comfortable with doing yoga, simple neck stretches and head rolls can open this chakra, release tension, and improve the flow of energy to the throat and neck. Practice neck stretches by leaning your ears toward your shoulders on each side and by slowly rolling your head clockwise and counterclockwise. Breathe deeply and practice these with mindfulness and intention.

throat chakra affirmations

I speak my truth.

My voice is my power.

It's safe for me to express myself.

I am safe to trust myself.

I am honest with myself and others.

I am clear and concise in my communications.

I have a patient and attentive nature when it comes to listening.

I take accountability for my actions.

I can safely communicate my feelings with others.

I have the ability to control which conversations I choose to participate in.

I am allowed to speak up.

I have meaningful things to share and contribute.

I am leading a life that is honest and true to myself.

The world is in need of me because I bring unique value.

I choose authenticity over perfection.

The answers I seek are within me.

I am unafraid to ask for what I want.

I have complete trust that my healthy boundaries can protect me.

more ways to support the throat chakra

essential oils Oils such as lavender, chamomile, eucalyptus, frankincense, and tea tree help balance the throat chakra by encouraging mental clarity, self-expression, and calmness.

sound healing Vibrational practices such as sound healing can have a harmonizing effect on this chakra. Try a sound bath or singing crystal bowl session.

sing or practice vocal exercises Activate the fifth chakra through vocal exercises like singing, chanting, or humming. You can chant the throat chakra mantra, which is "Ham" (*ha-n-gm*), to target the vishuddha.

engage in public speaking To open and balance the throat chakra, try engaging in public speaking. If you're new to this, start by picking a subject you know very well to build self-confidence and practice clearly articulating. Join a Toastmasters club or volunteer your knowledge at a local school or library. If you need some courage, keep a throat chakra–supporting crystal on you.

set clear boundaries Setting boundaries is a way of honoring and respecting yourself as you establish clear communication. If you need help in this area, I recommend the book *Set Boundaries, Find Peace: A Guide to Reclaiming Yourself* by Nedra Glover Tawwab.

third eye chakra

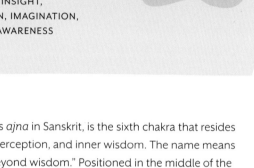

sanskrit name
AJNA

element
LIGHT

location
BETWEEN THE EYEBROWS
(FOREHEAD)

characteristics
INTUITION, INSIGHT,
PERCEPTION, IMAGINATION,
SPIRITUAL AWARENESS

color
INDIGO

The third eye chakra, known as *ajna* in Sanskrit, is the sixth chakra that resides within the realm of intuition, perception, and inner wisdom. The name means "perceive," "command," or "beyond wisdom." Positioned in the middle of the forehead, just above the space between the eyebrows, the ajna is often referred to as the "brow chakra" and is associated with the pituitary gland, pineal gland, brain, eyes, and central nervous system.

The element linked to the third eye chakra is light, which provides us with the ability to see by illuminating the world around us. The ajna chakra represents our ability to tap into our intuition, visualize, and gain insight that transcends the physical world. It guides us to perceive higher truths and foster a deeper understanding of the universe and ourselves.

Balancing the third eye chakra encourages us to listen to our inner voice, trust our instincts, and seek deeper meaning in life. Those with a harmonious sixth chakra experience enhanced creativity, mental clarity, and vivid imagination. They are able to clearly remember their dreams, follow their "gut instincts," and feel a sense of life purpose. This chakra opens the doorway to heightened spiritual awareness and facilitates the connection between our higher self and universal consciousness.

Conversely, an imbalanced or blocked third eye chakra can result in mental fog, confusion, and a lack of clarity in decision-making. An overactive sixth chakra is linked to excessive daydreaming or escapism from reality, while those with an underactive third eye chakra exhibit skepticism and lack of intuition. Physical symptoms such as headaches, vision issues, and sleep disturbances are also believed to be linked to an imbalanced sixth chakra.

Thankfully, we can easily feed the third eye chakra with food that encourages brain, mood, and sleep health to support overall cognitive function and mental clarity. As with the throat chakra, we can also benefit the third eye by mindful and intuitive eating to cultivate a deeper sense of connection and awareness.

feeding your third eye chakra

To balance the third eye chakra, we can feed it with adaptogens, vibrant purple produce, and foods to support sleep, brain, and mood health.

foods to support sleep health

No stranger to the subject of sleep, I have written several pieces on how food affects sleep, including recipes and meal plans, on Sleep.com. Sleep is essential to optimal function in regard to so many areas of health and well-being. Sleep health supports the third eye chakra by powering the brain to think clearly and perform effectively. Moreover, the pineal gland, commonly referred to as the third eye, is responsible for secreting the hormone melatonin. This hormone plays a vital role in controlling the sleep-wake cycle and maintaining the body's circadian rhythms.

Studies have noted that a minimum of seven hours of sleep each night is necessary for proper cognitive and behavioral function. This is crucial because a well-balanced third eye is linked to enhanced dream recall, more vivid dreams, and a deeper connection to the subconscious mind.

Food impacts sleep in numerous ways. Nutrients, enzymes, amino acids, and hormones—whether found in or produced by the foods we eat—all work to regulate sleep cycles. Some of these foods include tart cherries, which have above-average concentrations of melatonin; magnesium-rich foods like almonds;

foods high in tryptophan, such as turkey and dairy; and foods that increase the production of serotonin, such as dark chocolate, leafy greens, fermented foods, and sources of omega-3 fatty acids.

foods to support brain health and mood

In addition to supporting sleep health, foods can boost brain function and aid in mental health and mood. A clear mind is essential for balancing the sixth chakra, and enhanced focus can benefit many third eye-supporting practices, such as meditation. Foods to increase cognitive function include fatty fish, dark chocolate, blueberries, nuts, adaptogens (more in the next section), and stimulants such as coffee and green tea.

Green tea contains the amino acid L-theanine, which balances the caffeine to help you feel both calm and alert. Green tea has been shown to improve alertness, performance, memory, and focus. Chocolate, which contains both caffeine and flavonoids, has been studied to have similar effects on cognition.

Besides boosting brain power, certain foods can affect mental health and mood. This is due to the gut-brain axis we discussed in the solar plexus section (page 33) as well as the production of neurotransmitters from foods contributing to the production of mood regulators like serotonin. Studies have shown foods rich in omega-3s (e.g., salmon) and fermented foods (e.g., yogurt) to be among the top foods to support mental health and mood.

adaptogens

Common in Ayurvedic medicine, adaptogens are various herbs, plants, and mushrooms that support the body's ability to maintain balance or homeostasis in times of physical or emotional stress. Certain adaptogens—such as rhodiola, ginseng, maca, and adaptogenic mushrooms—have also been shown to enhance energy, focus, performance, and cognitive health.

purple foods

Resonating with the third eye's color, purple foods can feed our ajna. Like blue foods, purple foods receive their natural color from the plant pigment anthocyanins. In line with all antioxidants, anthocyanins can help neutralize harmful free radicals in the body and prevent various chronic diseases. The special thing about purple foods (including blue-purple and red-purple hues) is that they are known for their brain-boosting properties due to their unique combination of phytonutrients.

Take blueberries, for example, which have been shown to improve the communication between brain cells, memory, and cognitive processes. Similarly, other purple foods like açaí berries, eggplant, and grapes have been shown to protect the brain from damage as you age, boost cognition, and help prevent Alzheimer's disease.

list of third eye chakra foods

Foods to Support Sleep Health

Almonds
Banana
Barley
Chamomile tea
Chia seeds
Chickpeas
Citrus fruits
Eggs
Fig
Flax seeds
Grapes
Honey
Kiwi
Leafy greens
Milk and dairy
Mushroom
Oats
Passionflower tea
Pistachios
Raspberries
Salmon
Tart cherries
Turkey
Walnuts
Whole grains
Yogurt

Foods to Support Brain Health & Mood

Avocado
Banana
Beans and lentils
Beet
Berries
Blueberries
Bone broth
Broccoli
Cacao
Celery
Coconut oil
Coffee
Dark chocolate
Dates
Eggs
Fatty fish
Fermented foods
Green tea
Leafy greens
Nuts and seeds
Oats
Olive oil
Orange
Pumpkin seeds
Rosemary
Turmeric
Whole grains

Adaptogens

Ashwagandha
Astragalus root
Chaga
Cordyceps
Eleuthero
Ginseng
Gotu kola
Licorice root
Lion's mane
Maca
Moringa
Reishi
Rhodiola rosea
Schisandra berry
Shatavari
Tulsi (holy basil)
Turmeric

Purple Foods

Açaí berries
Blackberries
Butterfly pea flowers
Eggplant
Elderberries
Fig
Forbidden rice
Grapes
Lavender
Okinawan sweet potato
Passion fruit
Plum
Purple asparagus
Purple barley
Purple basil
Purple cabbage
Purple carrot
Purple cauliflower
Purple garlic
Purple mangosteen
Purple potato
Purple star apple
Radicchio
Raisins
Redbor kale
Red dragon fruit
Royal burgundy green beans
Ube
Ulluco

third eye chakra meal plan examples

	Breakfast	Lunch	Dinner	Snack
MONDAY	Build-Your-Own Savory Breakfast Bowls (page 114)	Amethyst Barley and Lentil Salad (page 118)	Blueberry Balsamic Salmon (page 147) served with forbidden rice	Adaptogenic Energy Bites (page 168)
TUESDAY	Chocolate Cherry Chia Pudding (page 106)	Roasted Purple Cauliflower Soup (page 130)	Roasted Eggplant with Tahini and Pomegranate (page 155)	Chocolate-Dipped Stuffed Dates (page 175)
WEDNESDAY	Hawaiian Açaí Bowls (page 100)	Hearty Vegetarian Chili (page 158)	Mediterranean Mezze Bowls with Quinoa (page 152)	Salted Honey and Maca Fudge (page 172)
THURSDAY	Oatmeal topped with blackberries, bananas, and chia seeds	Whole wheat spinach wrap with turkey, sliced tomato, and avocado	Sautéed fish served with purple sweet potatoes and steamed kale	Baked Beet Chips with Labneh Za'atar Dip (page 179)
FRIDAY	Omelet served with turkey sausage and fresh figs	Roasted beet salad with arugula and walnuts	Mushroom and barley soup served with a side salad	Purple grapes or fresh figs served with a cup of Meditation Tea (page 89)

third eye chakra crystals

Use the following crystals to inspire intuition, calm the mind, and boost spiritual awareness to support the third eye chakra:

 amethyst This sparkling stone is a powerful tool in supporting the opening and balancing of both the third eye and crown chakras. Amethyst is believed to enhance spiritual awareness, psychic abilities, and intuition.

 azurite Known as the "Stone of Heaven," azurite exhibits a rich, captivating color and vitreous luster. This powerful third eye–supporting stone promotes inner vision, spiritual awareness, transformation, and growth.

 iolite Named after the ancient Greek word for "violet," this gem is rich in striking purple and blue hues. Iolite, used to promote inner vision and wisdom, is believed to enhance sleep states and encourage more vivid, meaningful dreams.

 labradorite Associated with mysticism, magic, and intuition, this stone is known for its iridescent display of multiple vibrant colors. Labradorite aligns with the throat, third eye, and crown chakras, promoting self-discovery, communication, and spiritual growth.

 purple fluorite Known for its ability to promote mental clarity and spiritual awakening, purple fluorite can be a helpful tool in meditation. Fluorite comes in a wide range of colors, and this purple variety can support both the sixth and seventh chakras.

third eye yoga poses

Practice the following yoga poses to promote relaxation, encourage mindfulness, and help you balance your third eye chakra:

bee's breath (bhramari pranayama) This calming breathing exercise can soothe the nervous system, calm the mind, and induce sound sleep. To do this exercise, close your eyes and block your ears by gently pressing your thumbs over your ears. As you exhale, make a continuous humming sound that resembles the gentle buzz of a bee. Relax and focus.

candle gazing (trataka) Candle gazing meditation may help improve cognitive function and enhance spiritual connectedness. To do this meditation, find a quiet place where you can sit comfortably without distractions. Set a candle out in front of you at eye level and light it. Focus your gaze on the flame as you concentrate and quiet the mind.

child's pose (balasana) Child's pose is a relaxing and simple resting position that calms the mind to promote clarity and introspection. To practice this pose, kneel on the floor and sit back on your heels. Spread your knees about as wide as your hips and touch your big toes together. Bring your chest down to the ground and surrender to the weight of your body. Rest your forehead on the floor and keep your arms either at your sides or extended in front of you. Take deep breaths to calm your mind.

lotus pose (padmasana) Activate your third eye chakra with this pose, named after the lotus flower, which represents spiritual growth. To begin, sit cross-legged and bring each foot to rest on the opposite thigh. Stretch your spine toward the sky and lower your head toward your chest. Bring your hands together in the prayer position and place them in front of the third eye. Breathe deeply and clear your mind.

wide-legged forward fold (prasarita padottanasana) Create some space and awareness in your third eye chakra with this forward bend that stretches and strengthens. Stand with your feet wide apart as you gently hinge at your hips and fold forward. Rest the crown of your head on the ground as you increase blood flow to the head and allow this pose to cultivate a sense of introspection.

third eye chakra affirmations

I trust my intuition.

I am present in my life.

I am open to and enthusiastic about embracing new experiences.

I welcome fresh perspectives and ideas.

I seek to understand and learn from my life experiences.

I am connected to the universe.

I trust that my highest good is unfolding.

I honor my inner wisdom.

I can manifest my dreams and vision.

I am entering into a newfound sense of awareness.

I am a channel for inspiration.

I am in tune with my inner guide.

I am open to receiving guidance.

I am in touch with my spiritual truth.

I appreciate the beauty and enchantment that exists in my surroundings.

I am aligned with the path of my soul.

more ways to support the third eye chakra

essential oils To support the third eye, use oils that promote clarity and intuition, like frankincense, sandalwood, lavender, rosemary, and clary sage.

start a dream journal Record and decipher your dreams by starting a dream journal. Dreams can serve as a conduit for spiritual experiences, symbolic insights, and guidance. Writing down your dreams can be a helpful tool for exploring hidden aspects of yourself, uncovering patterns, and gaining a deeper understanding of the messages your inner self may be trying to convey.

don't be afraid of the dark Welcoming and exploring dark spaces is said to open the third eye chakra. To practice this, try meditating in a room only lit by candlelight or go stargazing in nature.

tap into your intuition with divination tools You can learn about and explore using divination tools such as tarot cards, oracle cards, and pendulums to amplify intuition, connect to higher guidance, and access the subconscious mind.

practice mindful meditation Meditation is an essential tool for the higher chakras. To enhance your third eye, focus your attention on the area between your eyebrows and visualize a vibrant indigo light expanding and enhancing your intuitive capabilities.

crown chakra

sanskrit name
SAHASRARA

location
TOP OF THE HEAD

color
VIOLET OR WHITE

element
THOUGHT

characteristics
SPIRITUAL CONNECTION,
DIVINE WISDOM,
ENLIGHTENMENT, ONENESS,
COSMIC CONSCIOUSNESS

Residing at the top of the head, the crown chakra is the seventh and final chakra. Its Sanskrit name, *sahasrara*, means "thousand" or "infinite" and this chakra is commonly referred to as the "thousand-petaled lotus." It is said that each petal of the lotus can represent a different aspect of our being or consciousness. The complete opening of all petals, or opening of the crown chakra, causes a universal alignment of the body, mind, and spirit.

The crown chakra transcends the physical realm and represents our connection to the universe and the divine. The element here is thought or consciousness, which symbolizes the highest level of awareness. The crown chakra is associated with two colors, violet and white, both of which depict purity, spirituality, divine wisdom, and transcendence.

Balancing the seventh chakra leads to a sense of oneness and deep spiritual insight. Opening the crown chakra unlocks the door to experiencing transcendental states of consciousness, the profound understanding of universal truths, and a sense of unity with all living beings.

An imbalanced or blocked crown chakra can manifest in feelings of disconnection from a higher purpose or a sense of meaning in life and spiritual stagnation. If you have an overactive crown chakra, you may be too disconnected from the physical world or your body. Some individuals may have an excessive focus on the metaphysical realm, leading to disorientation, headaches, and sensitivity to light and sound.

It is not recommended to work with the crown chakra until all of the lower six chakras are balanced. This will create holistic balance in the energetic body and also keep you grounded as you heighten your spiritual awareness.

feeding your crown chakra

Since the crown chakra transcends the physical realm and physical body, this chakra is not connected to food. The seventh chakra is actually related to the absence of food, or fasting, which is practiced in many religious and spiritual traditions. Buddhism, Christianity, Islam, Judaism, Jainism, and Hinduism are some of the religions and philosophies that engage in fasting, which can range in lengths and times.

There are various health concerns when it comes to fasting, and I am not suggesting fasting by any means. Always speak to your healthcare professional before attempting a cleanse or fasting routine.

When it comes to feeding and balancing all the chakras, consuming nutrient-rich and clean, unprocessed foods can support the body and mind. I do include a few detoxifying and cleansing recipes in this book, in addition to my favorite tea to enhance clarity and centeredness, Meditation Tea (page 89).

crown chakra crystals

Use the following crystals to encourage enlightenment and spiritual connection to support the crown chakra:

 celestite Possessing strong ethereal energy, celestite is known for its ability to connect the crown chakra and the angel realms. This calming light blue stone can enhance spiritual communication and promote inner peace.

 charoite Promoting a sense of divine guidance, this purple gem balances all of the upper chakras. Known as a powerful "soul stone," charoite can aid in purification, spiritual transformation, and inner vision.

 clear quartz Known for its ability to enhance other stones, clear quartz is a versatile crystal that can be used to balance all seven chakras. Its pure energy can support spiritual connection and higher consciousness.

 howlite This cream-colored and silver-veined stone is often used to support meditation practices and enhance mental clarity. Promoting a sense of tranquility, howlite is also beneficial for sleep, reducing anxiety, and promoting patience.

 selenite Known for providing clarity of the mind, selenite can clear blockages and facilitate a stronger connection to the higher self. Selenite, with its luminous white appearance, is often seen as a symbol of purity and spiritual illumination.

crown chakra yoga poses

Practice the following yoga poses to promote a sense of openness throughout the body, calm the mind, and balance the crown chakra:

alternate nostril breathing (nadī shodhana) This yogic breathing technique balances the crown chakra and promotes overall harmony. To practice alternate nostril breathing, sit comfortably and close your right nostril with your right thumb. Inhale deeply through your left nostril, then close your left nostril with your right ring finger while releasing your right nostril to exhale. Repeat this pattern, alternating nostrils with each breath.

corpse pose (savasana) This resting pose allows you to let go and release tension as you calm your mind and surrender to the earth. To practice this pose, lie flat on your back with your arms at your sides and your palms facing up. Close your eyes as you take intentional breaths and connect with your inner self.

meditation Any comfortable and secure yoga pose—such as easy pose, lotus pose, or seiza pose—will support your meditation practice. Meditation is a powerful tool for opening and balancing the crown chakra while connecting with your higher self.

rabbit pose (sasangasana) Open and balance the crown chakra with this surrendering, gentle inversion. To practice rabbit pose, start in a kneeling position with your legs resting on your heels. Reach your arms behind you, hold your heels, and gently fold forward as you lower the crown of your head to the ground.

third eye-supporting poses Additionally, all of the yoga poses in the third eye section (page 65) will support the crown chakra. Practice these to support both your sixth and seventh chakras and promote connection and enlightenment.

crown chakra affirmations

I am a spiritual being.

I am both guided and protected by the universe.

I am true to myself and embody my highest self.

I am aligned with my soul's truth and purpose.

I am able to find deep inner peace.

I let go of doubt and embrace faith.

The world serves as my teacher.

I embrace and submit to my highest good.

I live in harmony with nature.

I am willing to explore the depths of my own being.

My crown chakra is open and in perfect balance.

I am more than my ego-self.

I honor the divine within me.

I am fully present and awake.

I am connected to all.

I sense a profound connection to something greater than myself.

more ways to support the crown chakra

essential oils: Elevate your connection to the divine with essential oils that resonate with enlightenment and spiritual energy, such as frankincense, myrrh, lavender, and lotus.

explore sacred geometry: Discover the world of sacred geometry and mandalas to activate and balance your crown chakra. Creating or coloring mandalas can be a meditative practice that invites divine inspiration and a deeper understanding of how everything is interconnected.

explore astral projection and lucid dreaming: Delve into the realms of astral projection and lucid dreaming as tools to expand your consciousness and access higher states of awareness.

engage in acts of selfless service: Practicing selfless service, or *seva*, is a way to transcend the ego and connect with the divine through compassion and kindness.

engage in spiritual study: Explore spiritual teachings, sacred texts, and philosophical concepts that resonate with your understanding of the divine. Learning from different traditions can broaden your spiritual perspective and elevate your consciousness.

PART II

recipes

Healthful Food to Support Your Chakras

stocking your chakra kitchen

Stock your kitchen with the basics: rainbow produce, healthy fats, proteins, and whole grains. This will be the foundation of your healthful chakra-supporting diet. Once comfortable, you can add a variety of superfood ingredients to experiment with and invest in some helpful kitchen tools.

Animal-Based Proteins
Beef
Cheese
Eggs
Fish
Kefir
Milk
Poultry
Seafood
Wild game
Yogurt

Plant-Based Proteins
Beans
Buckwheat
Green peas
Lentils
Nutritional yeast
Nuts
Oats
Quinoa
Seeds
Soy-based proteins (tofu, tempeh, edamame)
Spelt
Spirulina
Wild rice

Fruits
Apples
Bananas
Berries (strawberries, blueberries, blackberries, raspberries, etc.)
Cherries
Citrus (orange, lemon, lime, grapefruit, etc.)
Dates
Dried cranberries
Figs
Freeze-dried fruit
Grapes
Kiwis
Mangoes
Melon
Peaches
Pears
Pineapple
Plums
Pomegranate
Pumpkin
Tomatoes
Watermelon

Vegetables
Artichoke
Asparagus
Broccoli
Brussels sprouts
Cabbage
Cauliflower
Celery
Cucumbers
Eggplant
Garlic
Green beans
Greens (lettuce, kale, spinach, dandelion, etc.)
Lemongrass
Onions, shallot, and leeks
Peppers
Potatoes and sweet potatoes
Rhubarb
Root vegetables (carrots, beets, parsnips, jicama, radish, lotus, etc.)
Sea vegetables
Squash (zucchini, butternut, acorn, spaghetti, etc.)

Whole Grains

Amaranth
Barley
Buckwheat
Bulgar
Corn
Farro
Freekeh
Millet
Oats
Quinoa
Rice
Spelt
Whole wheat

Healthy Fats

Avocado oil
Avocados
Ghee
Nuts (almonds, walnuts,
   cashews, pistachios, etc.)
Olive oil
Olives
Seeds (sunflower, flax, chia,
   hemp, sesame, pumpkin, etc.)
Sesame oil
Unrefined coconut oil
   (in moderation)

Spices & Herbs

Basil
Bay leaves
Cardamom
Chili powder
Cilantro
Cinnamon
Cumin
Ginger
Mint
Nutmeg
Oregano
Paprika
Parsley
Thyme
Turmeric

Sweeteners

Agave
Coconut sugar
Honey
Maple syrup
Pure vanilla extract

Superfoods & Adaptogens

Açaí
Ashwagandha
Blue spirulina
Cacao nibs
Cacao powder
Maca
Matcha
Mushrooms (reishi,
   cordyceps, chaga, etc.)
Pitaya powder

Other Refrigerator & Pantry Staples

Almond flour
Coconut milk and
   coconut cream
Coconut water
Dijon mustard
Dried fruit
Fermented foods (kimchi,
   sauerkraut, miso, etc.)
Ground flaxseed
Kombucha
Nut butters
Nut milks
Rice paper
Tahini
Tamari or coconut aminos
Vegetable, chicken,
   and bone broth
Vinegars (apple cider,
   balsamic, red wine, etc.)
Whole wheat or
   chickpea pasta

Helpful Kitchen Tools

Cast-iron and nontoxic skillets
Chef's knife
Cold press juicer
Cutting boards
Dutch oven
Fine-mesh strainer
Fish spatula
Food processor
Grater
High-speed blender
Mandoline
Measuring spoons and cups
Meat thermometer
Mixing bowls in various sizes
Parchment paper
Reusable food storage
   containers and bags
Sheet pans
Vegetable peeler
Zester (or Microplane)

a note on the recipes in this book

The recipes in *Feed Your Chakras* have been carefully developed and tested to help you nourish your body, provide balanced energy to the chakras, and taste amazing. Here are some notes on cooking from this book.

Recipes are tagged by the following diets or categories:

dairy-free Recipe contains no dairy or milk products from cows, sheep, or goats.

gluten-free Recipe contains no gluten, a protein found in wheat, barley, and rye.

grain-free Recipe contains no grains, including wheat, rye, spelt, barley, dry corn, rice, and oats.

one pan Recipe is made in one pan or dish from start to finish.

paleo Recipe follows a paleolithic diet which focuses on fruits, vegetables, lean meats, eggs, fish, nuts, and seeds.

quick & easy Recipe is made in 30 minutes or less, including prep work time.

vegan Recipe follows a vegan diet that excludes any animal, fish, or seafood proteins, as well as products derived from animals such as dairy, eggs, and honey.

vegetarian Recipe follows a vegetarian diet, which omits animal, fish, or seafood proteins but includes eggs and dairy.

All of the recipes in this book:

Are or can be made gluten-free. However, if you are following a strict gluten-free diet, ensure that certain ingredients featured in this book—such as oats, soba noodles, tamari sauce, or chickpea pasta—are certified gluten-free.

Use sugar in moderation. The recipes in this book contain no refined white or brown sugar. However, some recipes (especially desserts) use honey, agave, maple syrup, and coconut sugar in moderation.

Are customizable. Recipes can be made plant-based, dairy-free, or grain-free, and I include my best tips on how to do so whenever possible.

Are attainable. The recipes in this book are meant to be accessible, approachable, and easily incorporated into everyday life. The niche ingredients in this book—including butterfly pea flowers, spirulina, and pitaya powder—can all be ordered online if they can't be found at natural food stores or a local specialty grocer.

Encourage you to taste as you go. Tasting for seasoning is such an important factor when it comes to cooking. I do not provide exact measurements for salt or pepper in my recipes, unless they are a baking or dessert recipe or they cannot be tasted raw. This is because many people have different preferences and dietary needs when it comes to salt. I encourage you instead to taste as you go, seasoning each layer when cooking and adding more salt, pepper, spices, or acid to suit your tastes. Personalize these recipes and make them your own!

Turmeric Tea Three Ways

beverages

antioxidant berry smoothie

dairy-free · gluten-free · grain-free · paleo · quick & easy · vegetarian

chakra SACRAL; THROAT
serves 1
prep time 10 MINUTES

1 cup (240 ml) cold almond milk

1 tablespoon almond butter

½ frozen banana

½ cup (75 g) frozen mixed berries, plus more for garnishing

1 tablespoon ground flaxseed

¼ teaspoon ground cinnamon

1 teaspoon honey

1 teaspoon flax or chia seeds, plus more for garnishing

Fresh mint leaves, for garnishing (optional)

Drink this smoothie and your second chakra will thank you. Liquid foods are essential for balancing the water element of this chakra, while the addition of almonds, flaxseed, and cinnamon provide powerful sacral support. The antioxidant-rich foods found in this smoothie, such as berries, nuts, seeds, and cinnamon, protect the body from oxidative stress by defending our cells against free radicals.

1 Place all ingredients in a high-speed blender and process until smooth and creamy.

2 Top with additional seeds, berries, and mint leaves (if using).

did you know? There's a lot to love about flax, a small but mighty seed that's a good source of protein, fiber, and cancer-fighting lignans. To boot, the omega-3 fatty acids found in nuts and flax have been scientifically proven to promote brain health and reduce the risk of heart disease.

customize it Easily make this smoothie vegan by swapping the honey for agave or skipping it altogether.

turmeric tea three ways

dairy-free · gluten-free · grain-free · paleo · quick & easy · vegetarian

chakra ROOT; SACRAL; SOLAR PLEXUS; THIRD EYE; THROAT
serves 2 (PER RECIPE)
prep time 5–10 MINUTES
cook time 5–10 MINUTES

I am one of turmeric's biggest fans. From anti-inflammatory to anticancer to antioxidant benefits, there isn't much that turmeric and its active ingredient curcumin can't do. This is my go-to turmeric tea recipe, with different ways to switch things up seasonally. Sip an iced tropical version in the summer and a cozy pumpkin spice version in the winter and fall.

pumpkin turmeric tea latte

2 cups (480 ml) unsweetened vanilla almond milk

1 tablespoon honey, agave, or maple syrup

⅓ cup (75 g) 100% pure pumpkin puree

2 teaspoons coconut oil, melted

1 teaspoon ground turmeric

1 teaspoon ground cinnamon, plus more for garnishing

½ teaspoon ground ginger

¼ teaspoon ground nutmeg

¼ teaspoon ground allspice

¼ teaspoon ground cloves

Pinch of pepper

2 cinnamon sticks, for serving

1 In a small saucepan, whisk together the almond milk and honey. Bring to a simmer over medium-low heat.

2 In a blender, process the pumpkin puree, coconut oil, turmeric, ground cinnamon, ginger, nutmeg, allspice, cloves, and pepper until completely mixed with no lumps.

3 Once the almond milk is simmering, slowly pour ½ cup (120 ml) into the blender. Process, then stop, scraping down the sides with a spatula to ensure everything is incorporated. With the blender running, slowly add the rest of the almond milk, then process at high speed until frothy.

4 Divide between two mugs and serve with additional cinnamon sprinkled on top and a cinnamon stick.

iced tropical golden tea latte

1 In a small saucepan, whisk together the water, turmeric, pepper, ginger, and agave. Bring to a simmer over medium-low heat and whisk well to dissolve the spices. Set aside to let cool to room temperature. Once cool, remove the ginger.

2 Whisk the pineapple juice and coconut milk into the cooled mixture. Divide between two 16-ounce (475 ml) glasses filled with ice. Garnish with a pineapple slice and pineapple leaves (if using).

ingredient tip Don't skip the pepper. Research supports that pairing black pepper with turmeric enhances the absorption of curcumin by up to 2,000 percent!

1 cup (240 ml) filtered water

1 teaspoon ground turmeric

Pinch of pepper

1 piece (1 inch, or 2.5 cm) ginger

2 tablespoons agave

2 cups (480 ml) cold pineapple juice

½ cup (120 ml) coconut milk

Ice

2 pineapple slices, for garnishing

Pineapple leaves, for garnishing (optional)

turmeric tea latte

1 Warm all ingredients in a small saucepan over medium-low heat until it comes to a low simmer.

2 Whisk well to dissolve the spices and remove the ginger. Divide the tea between two mugs.

2 cups (480 ml) milk of choice (whole, coconut, almond, etc.)

1½ teaspoons ground turmeric

½ teaspoon ground cinnamon

1 piece (1 inch, or 2.5 cm) ginger

1 tablespoon honey, agave, or maple syrup

Pinch of pepper

kombucha wine spritzer

dairy-free · gluten-free · grain-free · quick & easy · vegetarian

chakra ROOT; SACRAL; SOLAR PLEXUS
serves 2
prep time 10 MINUTES

1 cup (240 ml) pinot grigio

½ cup (120 ml) berry-flavored kombucha (such as raspberry-lemon)

1 tablespoon fresh lime juice

Ice

Lemon slices, for garnishing

Orange slices, for garnishing

Handful fresh or frozen raspberries, for garnishing

Fresh mint, for garnishing

My best friend introduced me to the wonderful combination of wine and kombucha. If you've never tried it, it's incredibly refreshing and absolutely delicious. Not only do both wine and kombucha provide a rich source of antioxidants, but kombucha also offers gut-friendly probiotics. And for those who prefer not to consume alcohol, there is now a wide variety of nonalcoholic wines available to choose from.

1 In a small pitcher, stir together the wine, kombucha, and lime juice.

2 Fill two glasses with ice and divide the beverage between the glasses. Garnish with lemon slices, orange slices, raspberries, and a sprig of fresh mint.

variations

spiced red wine 1 cup (240 ml) red wine + ½ cup (120 ml) ginger kombucha + 2 tablespoons orange juice; garnish with orange slices and a cinnamon stick

strawberry rosé 1 cup (240 ml) rosé wine + ½ cup (120 ml) strawberry kombucha; garnish with fresh strawberries and lemon slices

sparkling watermelon basil 1 cup (240 ml) sparkling wine + ½ cup (120 ml) watermelon kombucha; garnish with fresh basil leaves and lime slices

blueberry kale
smoothie

dairy-free · gluten-free · grain-free · paleo · quick & easy · vegetarian

chakra THROAT
serves 1
prep time 10 MINUTES

1 cup (240 ml)
cold almond milk

1 cup (65 g) packed
chopped kale leaves

1 frozen banana,
halved

1½ cups (232 g) frozen
wild blueberries

1 tablespoon honey

1 teaspoon grated
fresh ginger

This delicious smoothie is the perfect way to add some extra greens to your day while supporting the throat chakra. Blueberries and kale are both very high in antioxidants, vitamin C, and vitamin K. One glass of this smoothie contains over 55 percent of your daily recommended amount of vitamin C and provides a generous dose of 9 grams of fiber.

Place all ingredients in a high-speed blender and process until smooth and creamy.

ingredient tip When it comes to blueberries, opt for wild ones when possible. Wild blueberries can easily be found in most grocer's freezer sections and contain more than double the antioxidant capacity of cultivated blueberries.

meditation
tea

dairy-free ◦ **gluten-free** ◦ **grain-free** ◦ **paleo** ◦ **quick & easy** ◦ **vegan**

This tea blend is excellent for supporting your third eye and crown chakras. Use this aromatic tea to encourage clarity and calmness and to enhance your meditation practice. Gotu kola, traditional in Ayurvedic medicine, boosts cognitive function and has a relaxing effect. The herbs found in this tea provide potent antioxidants, support brain health, and promote tranquility.

chakra CROWN;
THIRD EYE; THROAT
serves 20
prep time 5 MINUTES
cook time 15 MINUTES

¼ cup (30 g) dried
dandelion root

¼ cup (9 g)
dried gotu kola

¼ cup (7 g) dried
chamomile flowers

2 tablespoons
dried rosebuds

2 tablespoons
dried sage leaves

2 teaspoons
dried orange peel

Hot water

Ginger or lemon slice,
for serving (optional)

1 In a small bowl, stir together the dandelion root, gotu kola, chamomile, rosebuds, sage leaves, and orange peel until evenly combined. Transfer to an airtight container.

2 To prepare tea, use 1 tablespoon of the tea blend per 1 cup (240 ml) of hot water. Cover and steep for 10 to 15 minutes. Strain and serve with fresh ginger or lemon, if desired.

did you know? Making your own tea blends is easy, fun, and cost-effective. Some other herbs and ingredients to experiment with include peppermint, lemon balm, passionflower, lavender, catnip, and holy basil.

butterfly pea tea
color-changing cooler

dairy-free · gluten-free · grain-free · vegan

Butterfly pea flowers naturally color liquids a vibrant blue hue that turns a wondrous shade of violet when acid is added.

1 Add the dried butterfly pea flowers to a large bowl. Bring 4 cups (960 ml) of the water to a simmer in a small pot. Pour the water over the flowers and let them steep for 10 minutes, or until the water is a vibrant blue color.

2 Strain the flowers in a fine-mesh strainer set over a bowl, pressing down on them to release all the water. Reserve the water.

3 Divide the reserved water in half, pouring 2 cups (480 ml) into a container and transferring to the refrigerator.

4 Pour 1 cup (240 ml) unrefrigerated reserved water into ice tray molds. To the remaining cup (240 ml) unrefrigerated reserved water, add 1 tablespoon of the lemon juice to turn the water purple.

5 Pour the purple water into ice tray molds. Freeze the blue and purple ice cubes until set.

6 Once the cubes are set and you are ready to make the drink, bring the remaining 1 cup (240 ml) water, remaining ⅔ cup (160 ml) lemon juice, the agave, and ginger to a simmer in a small pot. Simmer for 2 minutes to dissolve the agave and infuse the flavors. Let cool to room temperature, then remove the ginger.

7 Divide the blue and purple ice among four 12-ounce (355 ml) glasses. Divide the chilled butterfly pea tea among the glasses. Divide the lemon syrup among the glasses, slowly pouring it on top of each drink.

8 Top each glass with sparkling water and garnish with a lemon slice.

chakra SACRAL; THIRD EYE; THROAT
serves 4
prep time 15 MINUTES
inactive prep time 4 HOURS (FOR ICE CUBES)

½ cup (14 g) loosely packed dried butterfly pea flowers

5 cups (1.2 L) filtered water, divided

⅔ cup (160 ml) plus 1 tablespoon fresh lemon juice, divided

3 tablespoons agave

1 piece (2 inches, or 5 cm) ginger

Lemon-flavored sparkling water, for topping

Lemon slices, for garnishing

customize it Make things easier and serve this cooler in a pitcher instead. Simply add the lemon syrup to a glass pitcher of the butterfly pea tea right before serving and allow guests to watch the mesmerizing color change.

detox vegetable broth
with ginger and turmeric

dairy-free · gluten-free · grain-free · one pan · paleo · vegan

chakra CROWN; ROOT; SACRAL; SOLAR PLEXUS
serves 8
prep time 10 MINUTES
cook time 90 MINUTES

1 gallon (3.8 L) filtered water

1 large onion, roughly chopped

1 medium leek, roughly chopped

4 cloves garlic, halved

3 medium parsnips, roughly chopped

1 bunch fresh parsley

½ head green cabbage, roughly chopped

1 piece (3 inches, or 7.5 cm) ginger, roughly chopped

3 ribs celery, roughly chopped

1 tablespoon ground turmeric

Sea salt

Homemade vegetable broth is easy to make and tastes far better than store-bought. This version is full of detoxifying and diuretic foods such as parsley, cabbage, and garlic, in addition to anti-inflammatory powerhouses turmeric and ginger. You may peel the onion, parsnips, and ginger or keep them unpeeled. Peeling the vegetables will give the broth a cleaner taste and appearance, but it is not necessary. Simply sip this soothing broth throughout the day or use it in your favorite recipes.

1 Combine the water, onion, leek, garlic, parsnips, parsley, cabbage, ginger, and celery in a large stockpot. Bring to a simmer over medium heat. Cover with a lid and let gently simmer for 1 hour and 30 minutes. Remove from the heat and stir in the turmeric.

2 Strain the liquid through a fine-mesh strainer into a pitcher and discard the vegetables. Store the broth in mason jars or airtight containers in the refrigerator for up to 1 week or freeze for up to 6 months.

ingredient tip You can save the vegetables you discard from the broth for another use. I will discard the parsley and ginger and keep the cabbage and vegetable mixture for a dinner side dish.

green glow juice

dairy-free · **gluten-free** · **grain-free** · **paleo** · **quick & easy** · **vegan**

Balance your heart chakra with this nutrient-packed green juice. Research shows that leafy green vegetables help reduce inflammation and heart disease risk. The ingredients in this juice also support cellular hydration and skin health, hence the "glow"! This juice is balanced, refreshing, naturally sweet, and perfect for anyone who is new to green juices.

chakra HEART
serves 2
prep time 15 MINUTES

3 or 4 kale leaves

1 medium lime, peeled

1 medium orange, peeled

1 medium cucumber

4 ribs celery

1 piece (1 inch, or 2.5 cm) ginger (optional)

2 medium Granny Smith apples, cored

Juice all produce according to your juicer's instructions, starting in the order of ingredients listed.

cooking tip No juicer? No problem. You can make this juice in a high-speed blender. Just peel and roughly chop all of the produce along with the juice from the lime and orange. Add cold water as needed to blend, then strain through a fine-mesh strainer or cheesecloth.

chia coconut water orangeade

dairy-free · gluten-free · grain-free · vegan

chakra SACRAL;
THIRD EYE; THROAT
serves 1
prep time 15 MINUTES
inactive prep time
4 HOURS (FOR ICE CUBES)

½ cup (120 ml)
orange juice, plus
more for ice cubes

1 tablespoon chia seeds

1 teaspoon agave
(optional)

1 cup (240 ml)
coconut water

Orange slices

Fresh mint, for garnishing
(optional)

This orangeade is one of my favorite beverages for so many reasons. First, it's incredibly refreshing. Second, it's packed with electrolytes, fiber, protein, vitamin C, and antioxidants. Last but not least, it supports multiple chakras thanks to brain-boosting chia seeds (third eye), juicy oranges (sacral), and soothing coconut water (throat). Move over, lemonade—this recipe may become your new go-to summer refreshment.

1 Make orange juice ice cubes by freezing orange juice in ice cube molds or trays until set.

2 Once the cubes are set and you are ready to make the drink, add the chia seeds, agave (if using), coconut water, and the ½ cup (120 ml) orange juice to a 16-ounce (475 ml) or larger glass. Stir well to combine. Let sit for 5 to 10 minutes to allow the chia seeds to expand.

3 Stir again and add the orange ice cubes and orange slices. Garnish with fresh mint (if using).

did you know? This chia drink can make an excellent post-workout option. Research has shown that because coconut water has tons of electrolytes such as potassium and magnesium, it's just as beneficial as sports drinks.

tropical bliss smoothie

dairy-free · gluten-free · grain-free · quick & easy · vegan

This delightful smoothie blends sweet tropical fruits and playful layering to support the second chakra. It offers two smoothies in one, allowing you to enjoy each layer separately or mix them together for a flavorful treat. If you want to focus on balancing the solar plexus, make the mango pineapple layer and enjoy it as a stand-alone smoothie.

---

1 To make the strawberry banana layer: Combine all ingredients for the strawberry banana layer in a blender and process until smooth. Divide between two glasses. Place in the freezer for at least 10 to 15 minutes.

2 To make the mango pineapple layer: Combine the ingredients for the mango pineapple layer in a blender and process until smooth.

3 Gently pour the mango pineapple layer over the strawberry mango layer in the glasses.

4 Garnish each glass with a pineapple slice.

prep tip Making smoothie freezer packs is a great way to prep in advance and save time. Place portioned cut fruit into individual freezer bags and when you're ready, simply add liquid and blend.

chakra SACRAL; SOLAR PLEXUS
serves 2
prep time 20 MINUTES

strawberry banana layer

½ frozen banana

1 cup (150 g) frozen strawberries, plus more for garnishing

1 kiwi, peeled and chopped

½ cup (120 ml) coconut milk

¼ cup (60 g) plain Greek or non-dairy coconut yogurt

mango pineapple layer

½ frozen banana

¾ cup (125 g) frozen diced mango

½ cup (125 g) frozen diced pineapple, plus more for garnishing

½ cup (120 ml) coconut milk

¼ cup (120 ml) orange juice

Sacral Sweet Potato Toast

breakfast

hawaiian
açaí bowls

dairy-free · gluten-free · quick & easy · vegetarian

chakra SACRAL;
THIRD EYE
serves 2
prep time 10 MINUTES

7 ounces (198 g) frozen
açaí puree (unsweetened)

1 cup (140 g) frozen
mixed berries

1 frozen banana

½ to 1 cup (120 to 240 ml)
cold apple juice, coconut
water, or milk of choice

Granola, for topping

Shredded or flaked
coconut, for topping

Sliced strawberries,
for topping

Sliced pineapple or papaya
for topping

*Living in Maui means that I am lucky enough to get an
amazing açaí bowl around almost every corner. Açaí
berries, known for their high antioxidant content, support
the sacral and third eye chakras. In fact, açaí berries possess
one of the highest antioxidant levels among all foods,
surpassing blueberries by threefold. These antioxidants and
plant compounds protect the brain against oxidative stress
and inflammation.*

1 Add the açaí puree, mixed berries, banana, and apple juice
to a high-speed blender and process until smooth. The
mixture should be very thick and creamy, so use the
smallest amount of liquid you need to process. Start with
½ cup (120 ml) and add more as needed.

2 Transfer the mixture to a bowl. Top with granola, coconut,
and sliced fruit.

customize it Top your bowl with your heart's desire: your
favorite fruit, nuts, seeds, nut butters, or even a layer of chia
pudding (page 104). For a protein boost, add a scoop of
protein powder before blending.

blue spirulina superfood
smoothie bowl

dairy-free · gluten-free · grain-free · paleo, quick & easy · vegan

Feed your throat chakra with vibrant blue superfoods. This creamy smoothie features a variety of fresh fruit, healthy fats, and superfood spirulina. Phycocyanin, the protein-binding pigment responsible for spirulina's color, is a powerful antioxidant that provides anti-inflammatory benefits. Additionally, spirulina—a good source of plant-based protein, B vitamins, and iron—has been shown to improve muscle strength, endurance, and energy levels. Now that's a breakfast of champions!

chakra THROAT
serves 1
prep time 10 MINUTES

1 frozen banana, halved

1 cup (150 g) frozen chopped mango

½ teaspoon blue spirulina

⅓ cup (80 ml) cold coconut milk

Dragon fruit, for topping

Blueberries, for topping

Blackberries, for topping

Unsweetened coconut flakes, for topping

1 In a high-speed blender, process the banana, mango, blue spirulina, and coconut milk until smooth, thick, and creamy.

2 Cut the dragon fruit in half and scoop out balls using a melon baller. Spoon the smoothie into a bowl and top with blueberries, blackberries, dragon fruit balls, and unsweetened coconut flakes.

did you know? Compared to green spirulina, blue spirulina has a milder taste that makes it a great addition to smoothies. Its slightly earthy flavor pairs well with fruit, especially tropical fruits, and fats like coconut milk.

customize it Add up to 1 teaspoon of blue spirulina to this smoothie. The smoothie will be a more vibrant, brighter blue with the more spirulina you add.

chia pudding
five ways

dairy-free · gluten-free · grain-free · vegetarian

serves 2 (EACH RECIPE)
prep and cook time
4 HOURS TO OVERNIGHT

Chia pudding is a versatile and easy breakfast that's packed with nutrients such as omega-3 fatty acids, protein, and fiber. Chia seeds are actually an impressive 35 percent fiber by weight. The combination of protein and fiber found in these small but mighty seeds can help you feel fuller for longer and ready to take on your day.

blueberry almond chia pudding

chakra THROAT

1 cup (155 g) frozen wild blueberries

1 cup (240 ml) almond milk

1 tablespoon maple syrup or honey

Pinch of ground cinnamon (optional)

½ teaspoon vanilla extract

¼ cup (40 g) chia seeds

Fresh blueberries, for topping

Sliced almonds, for topping

Fresh mint, for garnishing (optional)

1 In a blender, process the blueberries, almond milk, maple syrup, cinnamon, and vanilla until very smooth. Transfer the mixture to a medium bowl, then add the chia seeds and whisk well to combine. Let sit at room temperature for 10 minutes, stirring several times to ensure the chia seeds are well combined. Transfer to the refrigerator and let chill for at least 4 hours, or overnight.

2 When ready to serve, divide between two glasses and top with fresh blueberries and sliced almonds. Garnish with fresh mint (if using).

continued on page 106

chocolate cherry chia pudding

chakra ROOT; THIRD EYE

1 cup (240 ml) oat milk

3 tablespoons maple syrup, divided

2 tablespoons cacao powder

Pinch of sea salt

¼ cup (40 g) chia seeds

1 cup (155 g) fresh cherries, pitted and quartered, plus more for topping

1 tablespoon filtered water

½ teaspoon vanilla extract

Fresh mint, for garnishing (optional)

1 In a medium bowl, whisk together the oat milk, 2 tablespoons of the maple syrup, cacao, and a pinch of salt. Add the chia seeds and whisk well to combine. Let sit for 10 minutes, stirring several times to ensure the chia seeds are well combined. Transfer to the refrigerator and let chill for at least 4 hours, or overnight.

2 Add the cherries, remaining 1 tablespoon maple syrup, and water to a small pot over medium heat. Bring to a simmer and cook for 10 minutes, or until the cherries are soft and the liquid is thick and syrupy. Remove the pot from the heat and stir in the vanilla. Let cool completely.

3 When ready to serve, add a layer of chia pudding to each cup, followed by a layer of compote and then a second layer of chia pudding. Garnish with fresh mint (if using).

matcha raspberry chia pudding

chakra HEART

1 cup (240 ml) oat milk

1 tablespoon maple syrup or honey

½ teaspoon vanilla extract

2 teaspoons matcha powder

¼ cup (40 g) chia seeds

Fresh raspberries, for topping

Fresh mint, for garnishing (optional)

1 In a medium bowl, whisk together the oat milk, maple syrup, vanilla, and matcha. Add the chia seeds and whisk well to combine. Let sit for 10 minutes, stirring several times to ensure the chia seeds are well combined. Transfer to the refrigerator and let chill for at least 4 hours, or overnight.

2 When ready to serve, divide between two glasses and top with fresh raspberries. Garnish with fresh mint (if using).

peaches & cream chia pudding

1 In a medium bowl, whisk together the coconut milk, 1 tablespoon of the honey, vanilla, and cinnamon (if using). Add the chia seeds and whisk well to combine. Let sit for 10 minutes, stirring several times to ensure the chia seeds are well combined. Transfer to the refrigerator and let chill for at least 4 hours, or overnight.

2 When ready to serve, dice the peach and gently toss with the remaining 1 tablespoon honey.

3 Divide the pudding between two glasses and top with the honeyed peaches and whipped coconut cream (see **cooking tip**).

chakra SACRAL

1 cup (240 ml) light coconut milk

2 tablespoons honey, divided

½ teaspoon vanilla extract

Pinch of ground cinnamon (optional)

¼ cup (40 g) chia seeds

1 peach, pitted, for topping

Whipped coconut cream, for topping

Fresh mint, for garnishing (optional)

tropical coconut chia pudding

1 In a medium bowl, whisk together the coconut milk, yogurt, and agave. Add the chia seeds and whisk well to combine. Let sit for 10 minutes, stirring several times to ensure the chia seeds are well combined. Transfer to the refrigerator and let chill for at least 4 hours, or overnight.

2 When ready to serve, add a layer of chia pudding to each cup, followed by a layer of diced pineapple and then a second layer of chia pudding. Top with the sliced mango and coconut. Garnish with fresh mint (if using).

cooking tip Whipped coconut cream is easy to make and elevates any chia pudding (or dessert)! To make whipped coconut cream, place a can of full-fat coconut milk in the refrigerator overnight and then scoop out the hardened coconut cream. Whisk with a hand mixer until creamy, about 30 seconds, then add 1 tablespoon of sweetener of choice and ½ teaspoon of vanilla extract. Continue beating until it is fluffy, creamy, and forms soft peaks.

chakra SACRAL; SOLAR PLEXUS

¾ cup (175 ml) light coconut milk

½ cup (115 g) vanilla coconut yogurt

1 tablespoon agave

¼ cup (40 g) chia seeds

½ cup (85 g) diced pineapple, for serving

1 mango, peeled, pitted, and sliced, for topping

2 tablespoons shredded coconut, for topping

Fresh mint, for garnishing (optional)

protein-packed root vegetable hash

dairy-free · gluten-free · grain-free · one pan · paleo

chakra ROOT
serves 4
prep time 10 MINUTES
cook time 35 MINUTES

3 tablespoons olive oil, divided

2 fully cooked chicken apple sausage links, sliced

1 medium leek, white and light green parts only, halved lengthwise and thinly sliced

2 medium Yukon gold potatoes, peeled and diced

1 medium sweet potato, peeled and diced

1 medium parsnip, peeled and diced

1 small carrot, peeled and diced

Salt and pepper

2 cloves minced garlic

1 tablespoon chopped fresh sage, plus more for serving

1 teaspoon chopped fresh rosemary, plus more for serving

4 large eggs

This hash feeds your root chakra with protein and grounding root vegetables such as leek, gold potatoes, sweet potatoes, parsnips, carrots, and garlic. Chicken apple sausage and egg ensure a hefty serving of protein to start your day. This recipe highlights both the colors and the flavors of fall. It's a lovely dish to make to celebrate the autumn equinox, when we honor the harvest, Earth, and changing of the seasons.

1 Preheat the oven to 425°F (220°C).

2 Heat 1 tablespoon of the olive oil in a 12-inch (30 cm) oven-safe skillet over medium heat. Add the chicken sausage to the pan and cook until browned, about 5 minutes. Remove with a slotted spoon and set aside.

3 Heat the remaining 2 tablespoons oil in the pan over medium heat. Add the chopped leek and cook until just softened, but not browned. Add the gold potatoes, sweet potato, parsnip, and carrot. Stir to coat the vegetables in the olive oil and season with salt and pepper.

4 Cook the vegetable mixture for 15 to 18 minutes until tender, golden brown, and caramelized. Stir or flip frequently but give the vegetables enough time to brown.

5 Add the garlic, sage, and rosemary. Cook for 2 minutes, or until fragrant and the garlic is softened. Add the browned sausage back in and stir to combine.

6 Make four small divots in the hash and crack an egg into each one. Top the eggs with salt and pepper. Bake the hash in the oven for 6 to 8 minutes, until the egg whites are set and the eggs are cooked to your liking. Serve topped with additional fresh herbs, if desired.

Cooking tip Cut the vegetables roughly the same size to ensure even cooking and be sure to use a skillet that is at least 12 inches (30 cm) in diameter. The vegetables should have enough room to evenly cook and brown in a single layer.

Customize it To make this recipe vegetarian, simply omit the chicken sausage or replace it with your favorite plant-based sausage.

cinnamon apple quinoa porridge

dairy-free · gluten-free · quick & easy · vegan

chakra HEART; ROOT; SACRAL; SOLAR PLEXUS; THROAT
serves 4
prep time 10 MINUTES
cook time 20 MINUTES

1 cup (170 g) quinoa, rinsed and drained

2 cups (480 ml) unsweetened almond milk, plus more, warmed, for serving

1 vanilla bean

Pinch of salt

5 tablespoons maple syrup, divided

1 teaspoon ground cinnamon, divided

¼ teaspoon ground ginger

1½ teaspoons coconut oil

2 Gala apples, peeled, cored, and sliced

2 tablespoons apple juice

½ cup (60 g) pecans, chopped

ingredient tip Vanilla extract can be used in place of the vanilla bean. Stir in 1 teaspoon of extract when you add the maple syrup.

Tired of oatmeal? Switch things up with quinoa porridge. This delicious recipe supports multiple chakras with whole grains, heart-healthy foods, omega-rich fats, and warming spices.

1 Place the quinoa and almond milk in a medium pot over medium heat. Scrape out the vanilla bean seeds and add the seeds and the whole pod to the pot. Add the pinch of salt and bring the quinoa mixture to a simmer.

2 Once simmering, reduce the heat to low, cover, and keep the quinoa at a steady, low simmer for 15 minutes. Keep an eye on the pot to ensure it doesn't boil over.

3 At 15 minutes, remove the pot from the heat and let stand, covered, for 5 minutes, or until all the milk is absorbed.

4 Remove the vanilla bean and gently stir in 4 tablespoons of the maple syrup, ½ teaspoon of the cinnamon, and the ginger.

5 Heat the coconut oil in a medium skillet over medium heat. Add the apples, stir, and cook until softened and golden, 5 to 7 minutes.

6 Add the remaining 1 tablespoon maple syrup, remaining ½ teaspoon cinnamon, and apple juice. Stir to combine and cook until the liquid has evaporated, 2 to 3 minutes.

7 Scoop the quinoa into four bowls and pour your desired amount of warm almond milk over the top. Top each bowl with the apples and 2 tablespoons of the chopped pecans. Enjoy warm.

sacral sweet potato toast

dairy-free ▸ gluten-free ▸ grain-free ▸ paleo ▸ quick & easy ▸ vegetarian

Support your sacral chakra with sweet and savory sweet potato toast. This recipe boasts healthy omega-rich fats, protein, and fiber. Additionally, beta-carotene-rich sweet potatoes can enhance eye health and support the immune system. Select a sweet potato that is thicker and more rounded in shape.

chakra SACRAL
serves 4
prep time 10 MINUTES
cook time 20 MINUTES

1 large sweet potato, skin on

1 teaspoon olive oil, plus more for brushing and drizzling

Salt and pepper

1 avocado, peeled and pitted

1 teaspoon lemon juice

4 large eggs (over easy, fried, scrambled, or hard-boiled and sliced)

2 teaspoons hemp hearts

1 Preheat the oven to 400°F (200°C) and line a baking sheet with parchment paper.

2 Wash the potato very well and cut off the ends. Slice lengthwise into four ¼-inch (6 mm) slices.

3 Transfer the slices to the prepared baking sheet. Brush lightly with olive oil and season with salt and pepper. Bake for 20 to 22 minutes, until the slices are fork-tender and toasted, but not too soft or overcooked, flipping over halfway through.

4 In a small bowl, mash the avocado with the lemon juice and 1 teaspoon of olive oil. Season with salt and pepper.

5 Spread the avocado on the sweet potato toast and top with your egg of choice. Drizzle with additional olive oil and season with salt and pepper. Sprinkle each sweet potato with ½ teaspoon of hemp hearts before serving.

customize it To support the third eye chakra, swap orange sweet potatoes for purple. The anthocyanins found in purple sweet potatoes help support the brain by reducing inflammation and mental decline.

cranberry chai granola

dairy-free · gluten-free · one pan · vegan

This recipe thinks beyond tea when it comes to warming chai spices. Perfect for cooler months, this spiced granola is sweet, nutty, and fragrant. While it supports multiple chakras, the whole grains, complex carbs, and warming spices make it particularly beneficial for the solar plexus.

1 Preheat the oven to 300°F (150°C) and line an 18 by 13-inch (46 by 33 cm) baking sheet with parchment paper.

2 In a large bowl, whisk together the maple syrup, coconut oil, and vanilla. Whisk in the cinnamon, ginger, cardamom, and salt until evenly combined.

3 Next, stir in the rolled oats and almonds until evenly coated. Transfer the granola to the prepared sheet and spread in an even layer.

4 Bake the granola for 30 minutes, or until golden, stirring every 10 minutes. In the last 10 minutes of baking, add the cranberries and pumpkin seeds before stirring.

5 Remove from the oven and let the granola cool completely.

storage tip To store homemade granola, ensure the granola is cooled completely before transferring to airtight containers. It will last a few weeks at room temperature or up to 3 months in the freezer.

chakra ROOT; SACRAL; SOLAR PLEXUS; THIRD EYE
serves 8
prep time 10 MINUTES
cook time 30 MINUTES

½ cup (120 ml) maple syrup

¼ cup (60 ml) coconut oil, melted

1 teaspoon vanilla extract

1 tablespoon ground cinnamon

2 teaspoons ground ginger

1 teaspoon ground cardamom

Pinch of salt

2½ cups (225 g) rolled oats

¾ cup (105 g) whole almonds

⅔ cup (100 g) dried cranberries

¼ cup (56 g) pumpkin seeds

build-your-own
savory breakfast bowls

chakra HEART; ROOT;
SACRAL; SOLAR PLEXUS;
THIRD EYE; THROAT
serves 1
prep time VARIES
cook time VARIES

From whole grain breakfast bowls to savory oatmeal, there is nothing like a warm and satisfying meal to get you through your morning. I am someone who gets tired of eating the same things, so this formula is the perfect recipe to build different bowls based on your cravings or targeted chakra. It's also a great way to use leftovers. Choose your own chakra-supporting breakfast adventure!

bowl base (pick 1)

Cauliflower rice

Cooked brown rice

Cooked farro

Cooked quinoa

Prepared plain or cheesy oatmeal (any kind you like)

Roasted or mashed sweet potatoes

Roasted potatoes

Sautéed spinach or kale

protein (pick 1)

Chickpeas

Cooked chicken or turkey sausage

Cooked plant-based breakfast sausage

Egg of choice (boiled, fried, poached, scrambled, etc.)

Sautéed tofu

Smoked salmon

Tempeh bacon

vegetables & add-ins (pick 2 or 3)

Avocado

Fresh or sautéed greens

Marinated artichoke hearts

Roasted beets or eggplant

Sautéed mushrooms

Sautéed onions and peppers

Sautéed or steamed asparagus, squash, brussels sprouts, or broccoli

Sliced radish

Tomatoes

Zucchini noodles

sauces (optional)

Greek yogurt

Lemon hummus

Olive oil and fresh lemon juice

Garden Herb Pesto (page 121) or Kale Pesto (page 148)

Salsa or pico de gallo

Sriracha or hot sauce

Turmeric Tahini (page 136)

toppings (pick 1 or 2)

Cottage cheese or grated cheese

Fresh herbs

Hemp hearts

Nutritional yeast

Pumpkin or sunflower seeds

Sesame seeds or everything bagel seasoning

Sliced green onions

1 Add 1 cup (165 g) of your choice of base to your bowl.

2 Top with 3 ounces (85 g) of protein and your desired vegetables and add-ins.

3 Finish your bowls with a sauce (if using) and your desired toppings.

variations

heart chakra bowl 1 cup (150 g) cauliflower rice + sautéed tofu + 1 cup (130 g) sautéed kale + zucchini noodles + cherry tomatoes + sliced avocado + pesto (page 121 or 148) + pumpkin seeds

root chakra bowl 1 cup (225 g) roasted potatoes + 1 poached egg + 2 ounces (55 g) turkey sausage + sliced avocado + cherry tomatoes + sautéed mushrooms + Greek yogurt + sliced green onions

sacral chakra bowl 1 cup (225 g) mashed sweet potatoes + 1 fried egg + sautéed onions and orange bell pepper + baby spinach + olive oil and fresh lemon juice + hemp hearts

solar plexus chakra bowl 1 cup (200 g) farro or brown rice + 3 ounces (85 g) tempeh bacon + sautéed yellow squash + sautéed onions and yellow bell pepper + Turmeric Tahini (page 136) + sunflower seeds

throat chakra bowl 1 cup (234 g) prepared cheesy oatmeal + 3 ounces (85 g) chicken sausage + steamed broccoli + sliced avocado + Greek yogurt + everything bagel seasoning

third eye chakra bowl 1 cup (185 g) cooked quinoa + 2 ounces (55 g) smoked salmon + 1 hard-boiled egg + sautéed kale + sautéed purple potatoes or purple asparagus + fresh lemon juice + fresh parsley and dill

Chopped Greek Kale Salad

starters, soups & salads

amethyst barley and
lentil salad

gluten-free · vegetarian

Support the solar plexus chakra with whole grains and legumes and feed the third eye with rich purple produce. This salad is a potpourri of flavors and textures—combining soft, chewy, crunchy, fresh, savory, and slightly sweet elements. Powerfully aiding the third eye, ingredients such as almonds, barley, and honey support sleep while whole grains, lentils, and nuts boost brain health. Thanks to the anti-inflammatory antioxidants found in pomegranate, studies have shown this fruit can protect the brain against several cognitive diseases.

chakra SOLAR PLEXUS; THIRD EYE
serves 6
prep time 15 MINUTES

salad

1½ cups (236 g) cooked and cooled barley

2 cups (396 g) cooked and cooled green lentils

1 cup (40 g) thinly sliced radicchio

2½ cups (235 g) thinly sliced purple cabbage

1 large purple carrot, shredded

⅓ cup (12 g) chopped parsley

¼ cup (25 g) almonds, chopped

¾ cup (110 g) pomegranate arils, plus more for serving

¾ cup (115 g) crumbled feta, plus more for serving

vinaigrette

2 tablespoons pomegranate molasses

1 tablespoon red wine vinegar

1½ teaspoons Dijon mustard

1½ teaspoons honey

1 teaspoon lemon juice

½ cup (120 ml) olive oil

Salt and pepper

1 To make the salad: In a large bowl, gently toss the barley, green lentils, radicchio, cabbage, carrot, parsley, almonds, pomegranate arils, and feta until combined.

2 To make the vinaigrette: Whisk together the pomegranate molasses, vinegar, mustard, honey, and lemon juice. Slowly whisk in the olive oil until emulsified. Season with salt and pepper.

3 Toss the salad with half of the vinaigrette and reserve the rest for serving. Serve the salad topped with additional feta and pomegranate arils.

cooking tip You can cook both barley and lentils together in the same pot to save time. In a medium pot, combine ½ cup (100 g) pearl barley and 1 cup (190 g) lentils with 5 cups (1.2 L) water. Bring to a boil, reduce the heat to a simmer, and cook for 25 minutes, or until tender. Drain any excess water after cooking.

bone broth gazpacho

dairy-free · gluten-free · grain-free · paleo

This savory and refreshing no-cook soup is the perfect way to balance your root chakra. Rich in protein and bountiful with red foods such as tomatoes and bell peppers, this recipe takes classic gazpacho to a new level by adding nutrient-dense bone broth. Collagen-rich bone broth has been shown to protect the joints, maintain a healthy gut, and help support hair, skin, and nail health.

1 To make the gazpacho: Soak the shallot in the red wine vinegar for 10 minutes.

2 Blend the shallot, vinegar, tomatoes, cucumber, bell pepper, garlic, and lime juice in a blender and process until smooth.

3 Add the bone broth and process until desired consistency. Use less bone broth for a thicker soup. Season to taste with sea salt and pepper.

4 With the blender running, slowly pour in the olive oil to emulsify. Strain the gazpacho through a fine-mesh strainer and chill for at least 4 hours, preferably overnight.

5 To make the garden herb pesto (if using): Place all the ingredients in a food processor and process until just combined.

6 When ready to serve, top the gazpacho with diced cucumber and tomato. Drizzle with the herb pesto.

ingredient tip When it comes to gazpacho, choose the ripest and juiciest tomatoes you can find, and try using heirloom tomatoes when in season (late summer through fall).

customize it Make this gazpacho vegan by using a protein vegetable broth in place of bone broth.

chakra ROOT
serves 4
prep time 15 MINUTES
inactive prep time
4 HOURS

gazpacho
1 shallot, diced

2 tablespoons
red wine vinegar

2 pounds (1 kg) ripe Roma tomatoes, seeded and diced, plus more for serving

1 small cucumber, seeded and diced, plus more for serving

1 medium red bell pepper, seeded and diced

2 cloves minced garlic

Juice of 1 lime, or 2 tablespoons

1½ to 2 cups (360 to 480 ml) bone broth

Salt and pepper

⅓ cup (80 ml) olive oil

pesto
1 cup (40 g) packed mixed fresh herbs (such as basil, cilantro, parsley, and/or mint)

1 clove garlic, minced

1 tablespoon fresh lemon juice

2 tablespoons olive oil

Sea salt and pepper

rainbow summer rolls

dairy-free · gluten-free · vegan

chakra HEART; SACRAL; SOLAR PLEXUS; THROAT
serves 4–5
prep time 30 MINUTES
cook time 6 MINUTES

Served with a savory, protein-packed peanut dip, this vegan rainbow recipe is vibrant and refreshing.

dipping sauce
½ cup (130 g) creamy peanut butter

1 tablespoon rice vinegar

1 tablespoon sesame oil

2 tablespoons tamari

1 tablespoon fresh lime juice

2 tablespoons agave

1 teaspoon grated fresh ginger

1 teaspoon sriracha or chili garlic sauce (optional)

¼ cup (60 ml) hot water, as needed

Chopped peanuts, for topping

Sesame seeds, for garnishing

Cilantro, for garnishing

rolls
4 ounces (115 g) vermicelli rice noodles

1 teaspoon blue spirulina

½ to 1 teaspoon sesame oil

8 to 10 spring roll rice wrappers

1 large mango, peeled, pitted, and cut into thin strips

1½ cups (140 g) finely shredded purple cabbage

1 medium cucumber, seeded and cut into matchsticks

1 medium carrot, cut into matchsticks

1 medium red bell pepper, seeded and cut into thin strips

½ cup (20 g) chopped fresh cilantro

1 To make the dipping sauce: In a medium bowl, whisk together the peanut butter, rice vinegar, 1 tablespoon sesame oil, tamari, lime juice, agave, ginger, and sriracha, if using.

2 Add the hot water, 1 tablespoon at a time, until a creamy and saucy consistency is achieved. Transfer to a serving bowl and top with the chopped peanuts, sesame seeds, and cilantro.

3 To make the rolls: Prepare the vermicelli noodles according to the package instructions. Rinse the noodles under cold water and drain. In a medium bowl, toss the noodles with the blue spirulina until evenly colored blue. Toss with a small amount of sesame oil to prevent sticking.

4 Fill a shallow dish with room-temperature water. Working one roll at a time, gently place a rice wrapper in the water for about 15 seconds, or until soft and pliable. Move the wrapper to a damp surface or cutting board with a damp towel on top. Working quickly, stack the filling ingredients on the rice wrapper in a long narrow row, leaving 2 inches (5 cm) on either side. Start by layering the mango, followed by the cabbage, cucumber, carrot, bell pepper, noodles, and cilantro.

5 Fold the sides of the wrapper over the mound, then gently but tightly roll.

6 Cover the finished spring rolls in a damp paper towel until ready to eat. Cut in half and serve with the peanut sauce.

cooking tip Avoid overfilling the rolls, as this can result in tears in the rice paper or ingredients spilling out. It's best to err on the side of underfilling until you get used to making them.

dandelion greens salad
with strawberries and goat cheese

gluten-free · grain-free · quick & easy · vegetarian

Upgrade your spinach salad with the addition of dandelion greens, fresh strawberries, creamy goat cheese, and walnuts caramelized in coconut sugar and cinnamon. Dandelion greens are loaded with antioxidants, rich in chlorophyll, and a powerful heart chakra supporter.

chakra HEART
serves 4
prep time 15 MINUTES
cook time 5 MINUTES

caramelized walnuts

3 tablespoons coconut sugar

¼ teaspoon ground cinnamon

½ cup (60 g) walnuts, chopped

Pinch of sea salt

vinaigrette

¼ cup (60 ml) olive oil

2 tablespoons balsamic vinegar

1 tablespoon honey

½ teaspoon Dijon mustard

Salt and pepper

salad

3 cups (60 g) dandelion greens, chopped

3 cups (90 g) baby spinach

6 large strawberries, quartered

1 avocado, peeled, cored, and sliced or diced

⅓ cup (40 g) crumbled goat cheese

1 To make the caramelized walnuts: Line a small baking sheet with parchment paper and set aside. In a medium skillet over medium heat, heat the coconut sugar, cinnamon, and 3 tablespoons of water until bubbling and the sugar has dissolved. Once simmering, stir in the walnuts. Stir to completely coat the walnuts in the sugar mixture.

2 Cook the walnuts, stirring, until all of the water has completely evaporated. The mixture will be very sticky and sugar "strings" will form when stirring. Spread the walnuts quickly on the prepared baking sheet. Separate the walnuts as much as possible and sprinkle with sea salt. Let cool completely until hardened and set.

3 To make the honey balsamic vinaigrette: Shake all ingredients in a mason jar or whisk in a bowl until combined.

4 To make the salad: In a large bowl, toss the dandelion greens, spinach, and strawberries with the vinaigrette and transfer to a serving bowl or platter. Top with the avocado, goat cheese, and caramelized walnuts.

did you know? Opt for younger, smaller dandelion greens, which are less bitter than mature greens. Dandelion has a long history of use as a digestive tonic due to its bitter properties. Bitter foods like dandelion activate the liver and stimulate digestive juices, helping the body prepare to process food more effectively.

butternut squash and pear soup

dairy-free · gluten-free · grain-free · paleo

chakra SACRAL;
SOLAR PLEXUS; THROAT
serves 6
prep time 15 MINUTES
cook time 30 MINUTES

2½ pounds (1.1 kg)
butternut squash
with the seeds

3 tablespoons plus
1 teaspoon olive oil,
divided

Salt and pepper

1 medium yellow onion,
diced

2 stalks celery, diced

1 large carrot, diced

3 cloves garlic, minced

2 teaspoons minced
fresh ginger

2 Anjou pears, peeled,
cored, and diced

Pinch of ground nutmeg

5 cups (1.2 L) chicken broth

¼ cup (60 ml) full-fat
coconut milk, plus more
for garnishing

1 tablespoon chopped
fresh rosemary, plus more
for garnishing

This comforting recipe is a lovely way to warm up in crisp weather. Pear provides sweetness, coconut milk imparts creaminess, and root vegetables and aromatics add earthiness to this butternut squash soup. Beta-carotene-rich butternut squash is a powerful immune system supporter—another reason to enjoy this soup during cold and flu season.

1 Preheat the oven to 300°F (150°C). Line a baking sheet with parchment paper.

2 Peel and halve the butternut squash and scoop out the seeds. Rinse the seeds under cold water in a colander, removing the squash flesh, and pat the seeds dry. Toss the seeds in 1 teaspoon of the olive oil, salt, and pepper.

3 Transfer the seeds to the prepared baking sheet and roast for 20 minutes, or until lightly browned. Cool and set aside.

4 Cube the butternut squash.

5 In a deep soup pot, heat the remaining 3 tablespoons olive oil over medium heat. Add the onion, celery, and carrot and cook until softened, 5 to 7 minutes. Add the garlic, ginger, pears, and butternut squash. Season with salt, pepper, and nutmeg.

6 Add the chicken broth. Bring to a simmer and simmer for 25 minutes, or until all the vegetables are very tender.

7 Using a blender or immersion blender, puree the soup until completely smooth. Return to the pot and stir in the coconut milk and rosemary over low heat. Taste and adjust the seasoning as necessary.

8 Portion the soup into bowls and garnish with a swirl of coconut milk, additional rosemary, and the butternut squash seeds.

ingredient tip Save time by using precut butternut squash from the grocery store. You will need 2 pounds (1 kg) of squash. You can swap the roasted squash seeds for pepitas.

chopped greek
kale salad

gluten-free · grain-free · quick & easy · vegetarian

chakra HEART
serves 4
prep time 15 MINUTES

dressing

⅓ cup (80 ml) olive oil

3 tablespoons
fresh lemon juice

1 clove garlic, grated

1 teaspoon Dijon mustard

1 teaspoon honey

½ teaspoon dried thyme

½ teaspoon dried oregano

Salt and pepper

salad

5 cups (325 g) stemmed
and chopped lacinato kale

1 cup (145 g) cherry
tomatoes, halved

¼ cup (30 g) red onion,
sliced

½ cup (75 g) kalamata
olives, chopped

½ cup (150 g) marinated
artichoke hearts, chopped

1 medium cucumber,
seeded and chopped

1 can (15 ounces, or 425 g)
chickpeas

½ cup (18 g) chopped
fresh parsley

½ cup (75) crumbled feta

Chopped salads are one of my favorite ways to eat greens, especially more bitter greens like kale. While all green and lettuce-based salads support the heart chakra, this Greek cuisine–inspired version includes other heart-healthy ingredients such as fruity olive oil, kalamata olives, fresh tomatoes, and fiber-rich chickpeas.

1 To make the dressing: Add all ingredients to a mason jar and shake until combined and emulsified. Season generously with salt and pepper and set aside.

2 To make the salad: In a large bowl, add the kale, tomatoes, onion, olives, artichoke hearts, cucumber, chickpeas, and parsley. Toss with the salad dressing until evenly mixed.

3 Transfer the salad to a serving platter or individual plates and top with the crumbled feta.

nutrient highlight One serving of this salad contains over 30 percent of the daily recommended value of vitamin C. Research shows that vitamin C, a powerful antioxidant, may lower the risk of heart disease, boost immunity, and protect against various diseases.

customize it Easily make this salad vegan by skipping the feta and swapping honey for agave in the dressing.

cucumber seaweed salad

dairy-free · gluten-free · grain-free · quick & easy · vegetarian

Cucumber seaweed salad is also known as sunomono, a popular Japanese salad with a sweet and savory vinegared dressing. This no-cook side dish is easy to make, crisp, and refreshing. Seaweed, a powerful throat chakra supporter, is rich in nutrients and aids in proper thyroid function due to its high iodine content.

chakra HEART; THROAT
serves 4
prep time 20 MINUTES

2 tablespoons dried wakame seaweed

2 Japanese cucumbers

Salt

¼ cup (60 ml) rice vinegar

2 teaspoons tamari

1½ teaspoons sesame oil

1 teaspoon honey

Furikake, for topping

1 Rehydrate the seaweed in a bowl of cold water for 10 to 15 minutes. Drain thoroughly and squeeze out the excess water. Roughly chop into bite-size pieces.

2 Thinly slice the cucumbers and place in a bowl. Sprinkle the cucumbers with a generous amount of salt and let sit for 15 minutes to draw out excess water. After 15 minutes, use your hands to squeeze out as much water as possible from the cucumbers and transfer to a serving bowl. Add the seaweed.

3 In a small bowl, whisk together the rice vinegar, tamari, sesame oil, and honey. Add to the cucumbers and wakame and gently toss to coat. Season with salt, if needed. Serve topped with furikake.

ingredient tip When it comes to dried seaweed, a little goes a long way. Once rehydrated, dried wakame will expand over five times its size. Since it absorbs so much liquid, you may need to add extra water while the seaweed is rehydrating to ensure all of it is submerged.

roasted purple cauliflower soup

dairy-free · gluten-free · grain-free · vegetarian

serves 6
prep time 15 MINUTES
cook time 55 MINUTES

Cauliflower comes in a variety of beautiful colors, including purple. This creamy, savory soup focuses on the third eye with vibrant violet produce. Spiced crispy chickpeas provide a welcome texture for this velvety soup.

soup

1 head (1½ pounds, or 680 g) purple cauliflower, chopped

1 pound (455 g) purple or gold potatoes, peeled and diced

4 tablespoons olive oil, divided

Salt and pepper

2 shallots, diced

3 cloves garlic, minced

1 bay leaf

3 cups (720 ml) vegetable or chicken broth

1¼ cups (300 ml) coconut milk

Fresh thyme, for serving

crispy chickpeas

1 can (15 ounces, or 425 g) chickpeas, rinsed and drained

1 tablespoon olive oil

¼ teaspoon ground cumin

¼ teaspoon paprika

¼ teaspoon ground ginger

Salt and pepper

1 Preheat the oven to 425°F (220°C). Line two baking sheets with parchment paper.

2 To make the soup: In a large bowl, toss the cauliflower and potatoes with 2 tablespoons of the olive oil and season with salt and pepper. Spread on one of the prepared baking sheets and bake for 25 minutes, or until tender and golden brown, flipping once halfway through. Set aside and lower the oven to 400°F (200°C). Reserve a few florets for topping the soup later, if desired.

3 To make the crispy chickpeas: Pat the chickpeas dry and add them to a medium bowl along with 1 tablespoon olive oil, cumin, paprika, ginger, salt, and pepper. Toss until evenly coated. Spread on the second prepared baking sheet. Bake for 30 minutes, or until crispy and evenly brown, stirring halfway through to ensure even baking.

4 To finish the soup: Heat the remaining 2 tablespoons olive oil in a Dutch oven or large soup pot over medium heat. Add the shallots and sauté until softened, 3 to 5 minutes. Stir in the garlic and cook for another minute. Add the cauliflower, potatoes, bay leaf, and broth to the pot. Bring the broth to a simmer and let simmer for 15 minutes. Stir in the coconut milk. Taste the soup and adjust seasonings as needed.

5 Remove the bay leaf. Using a blender or immersion blender, puree the soup until completely smooth and creamy. If the soup is too thick, you can add more broth until your desired consistency is reached.

6 Ladle the soup into bowls and top with the extra cauliflower (if using), chickpeas, fresh thyme, and a drizzle of olive oil.

rainbow salad jars

dairy-free · gluten-free · quick & easy · vegan

No boring desk lunch here. Salad jars are already fun and convenient to eat, but this colorful version proves they can be just as visually appealing. This tasty salad is packed with fiber, plant-based protein, potassium, and essential vitamins. The recipe as written yields one jar/one serving, but it can be easily scaled up or down for convenient meal prep.

1 To make the vinaigrette: In a small bowl, whisk together the lemon juice, honey, and mustard. Slowly whisk in the olive oil until emulsified. Whisk in the pepper and salt.

2 To make the salad: Assemble the salad in wide-mouth 16-ounce (475 ml) mason jars. For jars, add 2 tablespoons of vinaigrette to the bottom, followed by the tomatoes, roasted peppers, corn, shredded carrot, cabbage, cucumber, quinoa, and spinach. When adding the spinach, pack and press down to fit.

3 Store salad jars in the refrigerator until ready to eat. Salad jars will keep in the refrigerator for up to 3 days. When ready to eat, shake the jar to distribute the dressing.

serving tip Greens are kept at the top of the jar to avoid contact with the dressing and to keep from getting mushy. Alternatively, you can prepare the salad jars without the dressing. When ready to serve, pour the mason jar contents into a bowl and toss with 2 tablespoons of the vinaigrette.

chakra HEART; SACRAL; SOLAR PLEXUS
serves SERVES 1 (1 JAR); DRESSING YIELDS 5 OUNCES (148 ML), OR 5 SERVINGS
prep time 15 MINUTES

vinaigrette
¼ cup (60 ml) fresh lemon juice

1 teaspoon honey

2 teaspoons Dijon mustard

⅓ cup (80 ml) olive oil

¾ teaspoon freshly ground pepper

Salt

salad
4 grape tomatoes, halved

2 tablespoons sliced roasted peppers

¼ cup (35 g) sweet corn

¼ cup (55 g) shredded carrot

¼ cup (25 g) shredded purple cabbage

¼ cup (35 g) diced cucumber

¼ cup (50 g) cooked quinoa

1 cup (20 g) fresh baby spinach

Roasted Eggplant with
Tahini and Pomegranate

mains

crispy caulifower pitas
with turmeric tahini

gluten-free · vegetarian

chakra HEART;
SOLAR PLEXUS
serves 4
prep time 15 MINUTES
cook time 30 MINUTES

pitas

2 pounds (910 g)
cauliflower, cut into florets

3 tablespoons olive oil

2 teaspoons ground cumin

1 teaspoon paprika

½ teaspoon coriander

½ teaspoon garlic powder

Salt and pepper

4 gluten-free pitas, warmed

2 Roma tomatoes,
thinly sliced

1 cup (44 g) spring greens
mix, for serving

Crumbled feta, for serving

Chopped fresh cilantro,
for serving

turmeric tahini

¼ cup (60 ml) tahini

2 tablespoons fresh
lemon juice

1 tablespoon olive oil

1 teaspoon ground turmeric

1 clove garlic, grated

2 to 4 tablespoons
filtered water, as needed

Salt and pepper

Complete with satiating healthy fats and anti-inflammatory spices, this recipe is loaded with flavor. A bold yellow sauce, warming spices, and whole grains support the solar plexus, while cruciferous cauliflower, olive oil, tomatoes, and spring greens support the heart.

1 Preheat the oven to 425°F (220°C) and line a large baking sheet with parchment paper.

2 To make the pitas: In a large bowl, toss together the cauliflower with the olive oil. In a small bowl, whisk together the cumin, paprika, coriander, and garlic powder. Sprinkle the spice mix over the cauliflower and toss to coat, then season with salt and pepper. Spread the cauliflower in a single layer on the prepared baking sheet and bake until tender and golden brown, 30 to 35 minutes, flipping over halfway through.

3 To make the turmeric tahini: Whisk together the tahini, lemon juice, 1 tablespoon olive oil, turmeric, and garlic in a medium bowl. Add the filtered water, 1 tablespoon at a time, until the sauce is a creamy consistency. Season with salt and pepper.

4 Cut the pitas in half to create two pockets. Fill the pitas with a few sliced tomatoes, some spring greens mix, and the roasted cauliflower. Drizzle on the tahini sauce and top with feta and chopped cilantro.

customize it Instead of pitas, this recipe can be turned into a bowl by serving it over your choice of grains or on its own. Make extra turmeric tahini and have it on hand for salads or a veggie dip. Use more or less water to control the thickness and texture.

miso salmon soba noodle bowls

dairy-free · gluten-free · grain-free

chakra ROOT; SACRAL; SOLAR PLEXUS; THIRD EYE; THROAT
serves 4
prep time 15 MINUTES
inactive prep time 1 HOUR
cook time 15 MINUTES

bowls

2 tablespoons white or yellow miso

5 tablespoons tamari or soy sauce, divided

2 tablespoons rice vinegar, divided

1 tablespoon maple syrup

1 teaspoon grated fresh ginger

4 skin-on salmon fillets (6 ounces, or 170 g each)

1 package (9.5 ounces, or 269 g) soba noodles

1 tablespoon sesame oil

1 cup (155 g) shelled edamame, for serving

Lime wedges, for serving

Chopped fresh cilantro, for serving

Thinly sliced radish, for serving

Furikake, for serving

continued on next page

Salmon packed with omega-3 fatty acids is a nutritious protein that supports multiple chakras, including root, sacral, throat, and third eye. The base for this colorful and flavorful bowl is buckwheat soba noodles. Buckwheat—rich in dietary fiber, protein, and antioxidants—has been shown to benefit blood sugar, heart health, and inflammation.

1 To make the bowls: In a small bowl, whisk together the miso, 2 tablespoons of the tamari, 1 tablespoon of the rice vinegar, maple syrup, and grated ginger. Place the salmon fillets in a shallow baking dish, pour the marinade on top, and marinate in the refrigerator for a minimum of 1 hour.

2 Let the salmon sit at room temperature for 15 minutes and preheat the broiler to high. Lightly grease a foil-lined baking sheet. Place the salmon on the pan, skin-side down. Broil for 8 minutes, or until the salmon is opaque, reaches an internal temperature of 125 to 135°F (52 to 57°C), and flakes easily with a fork. Let the salmon rest for 5 minutes.

3 To make the garlic mushrooms: Heat the olive oil in a medium skillet over medium-high heat. Add the mushrooms and cook until they are tender and browned, about 6 minutes. Add the garlic and cook for another 2 minutes. Stir in 1½ teaspoons tamari and cook for another minute. Season with salt and pepper.

4 To finish the bowls: In a large pot, cook the soba noodles according to the package instructions, rinse under cold water, and drain. Add the soba noodles back to the empty warm pot and toss with the remaining 3 tablespoons tamari, the sesame oil, and the remaining 1 tablespoon rice vinegar.

5 Divide the noodles among four bowls. Top each bowl with a salmon fillet. Divide the mushrooms among the bowls and add ¼ cup (40 g) of edamame to each bowl. Serve with lime wedges, chopped cilantro, thinly sliced radish, and furikake seasoning on top.

ingredient tip Despite its name, buckwheat is actually a seed, which makes soba noodles gluten-free. Read the package to ensure the noodles do not contain any added wheat.

garlic mushrooms

1½ tablespoons olive oil

8 ounces (225 g) cremini mushrooms, thinly sliced

3 cloves minced garlic

1½ teaspoons tamari or soy sauce

Salt and pepper

sheet pan chicken thighs
with roasted root vegetables

dairy-free · gluten-free · grain-free · one pan · paleo

Easy and convenient, sheet tray recipes are the ultimate one-pan weeknight dinners. This heart- and root-balancing recipe incorporates juicy marinated chicken, garlic, herbs, and tender earthy vegetables.

chakra HEART; ROOT
serves 6
prep time 15 MINUTES
inactive prep time
1 HOUR
cook time 40 MINUTES

1 In a large bowl, toss the chicken thighs with 3 tablespoons of the olive oil, lemon juice, garlic, thyme, oregano, Dijon mustard, salt, and pepper. Marinate in the refrigerator for 1 hour.

2 Preheat the oven to 425°F (220°C). Line a baking sheet with parchment paper.

3 In a large bowl, toss the brussels sprouts, potatoes, shallots, carrots, and beets with the remaining 2 tablespoons olive oil and the rosemary. Season with salt and pepper.

4 Transfer the vegetables to the sheet pan and arrange the chicken on top.

5 Bake for 40 minutes, or until the vegetables are tender and the chicken is golden brown and reads 175°F (79°C).

cooking tip If you want crispier chicken skin, place the tray under the broiler for 3 to 5 minutes after it is finished baking in the oven.

2½ pounds (1.1 kg) bone-in, skin-on thighs (about 6 thighs)

5 tablespoons olive oil, divided

2 tablespoons lemon juice, plus more for serving

2 cloves garlic, minced

1 teaspoon dried thyme

1 teaspoon dried oregano

1 teaspoon Dijon mustard

½ teaspoon salt

½ teaspoon pepper

2 cups (180 g) brussels sprouts, trimmed and halved

2 cups (220 g) baby potatoes, halved

4 shallots, quartered

2 medium carrots, cut into 1-inch (2.5 cm) pieces on the bias

1 medium beet, peeled and diced into ½-inch (1 cm) pieces

1 tablespoon chopped fresh rosemary

shrimp tacos
with grilled corn and pineapple salsa

gluten-free

chakra SOLAR PLEXUS; THROAT
makes 10
prep time 20 MINUTES
cook time 16 MINUTES

Who doesn't love a good Taco Tuesday? Elevate protein-packed shrimp tacos with a smoky, sweet, and spicy grilled corn and pineapple salsa to feed the solar plexus. This bright and zesty recipe is perfect for the summer grilling season.

grilled corn and pineapple salsa

2 ears corn

Olive oil, for brushing

1 cup (165 g) diced pineapple

¼ cup (31 g) red onion, finely diced

1 medium red bell pepper, seeded and diced

1 tablespoon fresh lime juice

⅓ cup (20 g) chopped cilantro

1 jalapeño, finely diced

Salt and pepper

tacos

1½ pounds (680 g) raw shrimp, peeled, deveined, and tails removed

1½ tablespoons olive oil

1 tablespoon lime juice

1 clove minced garlic

1 teaspoon paprika

1 teaspoon chili powder

½ teaspoon ground cumin

Salt and pepper

10 corn or flour tortillas, warmed

yogurt avocado sauce

1 ripe avocado, peeled and pitted

½ cup (115 g) Greek yogurt

1 clove minced garlic

¼ cup (10 g) chopped cilantro

3 tablespoons fresh lime juice

Salt and pepper

1 To make the salsa: Prepare a grill for medium-high heat. Brush the corn cobs with olive oil and grill for 10 to 15 minutes, turning occasionally, until the kernels are tender and slightly charred. Remove from the heat and let cool. Cut the corn kernels off the cobs and add to a large bowl. Add the pineapple, red onion, bell pepper, lime juice, cilantro, jalapeño, salt, and pepper and toss to combine. Set aside. Keep the grill going.

2 To make the tacos: Pat the shrimp dry with paper towels. Place the shrimp in a small bowl and add the olive oil, lime juice, garlic, paprika, chili powder, cumin, salt, and pepper. Thread the shrimp onto skewers and grill on a lightly greased grill for 2 to 3 minutes per side, until the shrimp are no longer opaque. Remove the shrimp from the skewers.

3 To make the yogurt avocado sauce: Process all the ingredients in a food processor or blender. If the sauce is too thick, thin it out with 1 to 2 tablespoons of water. The sauce should be the consistency of crema or sour cream.

4 Fill warmed tortillas with the shrimp and top with the salsa and sauce.

cooking tip To add an extra layer of flavor to the grilled shrimp, consider marinating them in the olive oil, lime juice, and spice mixture for 30 minutes before grilling.

green goddess
buddha bowls

gluten-free • vegetarian

chakra HEART; ROOT; SOLAR PLEXUS
serves 4
prep time 15 MINUTES
cook time 20 MINUTES

dressing

1 cup (230 g) whole milk Greek yogurt

1 cup (35 g) chopped parsley

½ cup (25 g) chopped dill

½ cup (20 g) chopped cilantro

2 tablespoons chopped mint

2 tablespoons lemon juice

1 tablespoon olive oil

1 clove garlic, minced

Salt and pepper

bowls

2 bunches (12 ounces, or 340 g) broccolini

2 tablespoons olive oil

Salt and pepper

4 cups (800 g) cooked brown rice or farro

1 cucumber, thinly sliced

1 cup (160 g) cooked shelled edamame

½ cup (75 g) pitted Castelvetrano olives

2 small avocados, peeled, pitted, and thinly sliced

1 cup (70 g) microgreens

¼ cup (35 g) pepitas

I love green goddess dressing and dreamed up this hearty bowl when I needed something more filling than a salad. It includes all of my favorite green foods—broccolini, crisp cucumber, edamame, creamy avocado, crunchy pepitas, and fruity Castelvetrano olives.

1 Preheat the oven to 425°F (220°C). Line a baking sheet with parchment paper.

2 To make the dressing: Pulse all of the ingredients for the dressing in a food processor or blender until combined. Refrigerate until ready to use. Dressing will keep in the refrigerator for 3 days.

3 To make the bowls: Cut the broccolini stems in half lengthwise and place them on the prepared baking sheet. Drizzle with the oil and toss to coat. Season with salt and pepper and spread the stems in a single layer. Bake until crisp-tender and slightly charred, 15 to 20 minutes, rotating the sheet halfway through.

4 Fill four large shallow bowls with 1 cup (200 g) of brown rice each. Divide the broccolini and cucumber among the bowls. To each bowl, add ¼ cup (40 g) edamame, 2 tablespoons of olives, half an avocado, ¼ cup (18 g) of microgreens, and 1 tablespoon of pepitas. Add the egg, if using (see **ingredient tip**). Drizzle with the dressing and serve.

ingredient tip Adding an egg will amp up the protein content of this bowl. To make the perfect soft-boiled egg, boil an egg in simmering water for 6 to 7 minutes before immediately transferring to an ice bath to stop the cooking process.

blueberry balsamic salmon

dairy-free · gluten-free · grain-free · paleo · quick & easy

Blueberries are not just for pie. If you've never tried blueberries in a savory recipe, now's the time. Blueberries pair beautifully with balsamic vinegar, thyme, lemon, and ginger and simmer into a thick sweet, savory, and acidic sauce to complement seared salmon. Supporting the sacral, throat, and third eye chakras, this recipe is loaded with protein, antioxidants, and omega-3s.

chakra SACRAL; THIRD EYE; THROAT
serves 4
prep time 10 MINUTES
cook time 15 MINUTES

1½ cups (220 g) fresh blueberries

8 sprigs fresh thyme, plus more for garnishing

¼ cup (60 ml) balsamic vinegar

2 tablespoons lemon juice

2 tablespoons honey

2 teaspoons grated fresh ginger

Salt and pepper

4 skin-on salmon fillets (6 ounces, or 170 g each)

2 tablespoons olive oil

1 In a small saucepan over medium-low heat, stir together the blueberries, thyme, balsamic vinegar, lemon juice, honey, and ginger. Season with salt and pepper.

2 Bring the mixture to a simmer. Stir frequently and simmer until the blueberries begin to break down and the liquid reduces to thicken the sauce, 12 to 15 minutes. Remove the thyme sprigs and set the sauce aside.

3 Pat the salmon fillets dry with paper towels and season with salt and pepper. Heat the olive oil in a heavy 12-inch (30 cm) skillet over medium-high heat until hot and shimmering.

4 Cook the salmon skin-side down, undisturbed, for 5 minutes, or until the skin is browned and releases easily from the pan.

5 Flip and cook the salmon on the other side until done to your liking, 2 to 4 more minutes. Salmon should be at an internal temperature of 125°F (52°C) for medium doneness, and will continue cooking as it rests.

6 Transfer the salmon to plates and top with the warm blueberry balsamic sauce. Garnish with fresh thyme.

serving tip

This salmon is delicious served with steamed haricot vert and quinoa or roasted potatoes. The lemon-herb quinoa from the Mediterranean Mezze Bowls (page 152) pairs wonderfully.

kale pesto pasta
with spring vegetables
gluten-free · grain-free · quick & easy

chakra HEART
serves 4
prep time 15 MINUTES
cook time 15 MINUTES

kale pesto

¼ cup (30 g) chopped toasted walnuts

1 clove garlic, chopped

2 cups (130 g) chopped kale, stems and ribs removed

½ cup (20 g) basil, plus more for serving

2 tablespoons fresh lemon juice

¼ cup (25 g) grated Parmesan, plus more for serving

¼ cup (60 ml) olive oil

Salt and pepper

pasta

8 ounces (225 g) chickpea rotini or penne

1 tablespoon olive oil

1 shallot, diced

2 cups (270 g) 1-inch (2.5 cm) pieces asparagus

¾ cup (100 g) fresh English peas

Salt and pepper

½ cup (120 ml) reserved pasta water

This green, veggie-packed pasta feeds your heart chakra with bright spring vegetables and earthy kale pesto. If you've never tried making pesto with fresh kale before, now's the time—this pesto is nutty, peppery, and fragrant with the perfect lemony punch. Superfood kale is rich in antioxidants, vitamin C, vitamin K, and beta-carotene. These essential nutrients not only promote eye, bone, immunity, and heart health but also provide protection against cancer.

1 To make the kale pesto: In a food processor, pulse the walnuts and garlic until finely chopped. Add the kale, basil, lemon juice, and cheese. Process until finely chopped and combined. With the food processor running, slowly add the olive oil until just combined. Season with salt and pepper.

2 To make the pasta: Cook the chickpea pasta according to the package directions in a pot of salted boiling water.

3 While the pasta is cooking, heat 1 tablespoon olive oil in a medium skillet over medium heat. Add the shallot and cook until softened, about 3 to 4 minutes. Add the asparagus and peas and cook for 3 minutes, or until just tender and bright green. Season with salt and pepper.

4 Drain the chickpea pasta, reserving ½ cup (120 ml) of the pasta water. Add the pasta to the skillet along with the pesto. Toss the pasta, vegetables, and pesto with the reserved pasta water, adding ¼ cup (60 ml) of pasta water at a time until the pesto is creamy and coats the pasta well.

5 Serve topped with additional cheese and chopped fresh basil.

ingredient tips Choose any type of pasta for this recipe. Even though chickpea pasta does not contain gluten, you can still use the starchy water the same way you would use traditional pasta water. Swap asparagus and fresh peas for broccoli and frozen peas when not in season.

storage tip Double (or triple) this kale pesto and use it throughout the week to top eggs, spread on sandwiches, garnish soups, dress veggies, or mix into Greek yogurt for a quick savory dip. Store leftovers in a glass jar and top with a thin layer of olive oil to keep the pesto fresh and green. It will keep in the fridge for up to 1 week.

orange sesame
tofu stir-fry

dairy-free · gluten-free · one pan · vegan

Brimming with vitamin C, this sweet and savory orange stir-fry supports multiple chakras with a strong connection to the sacral.

chakra HEART; ROOT; SACRAL; SOLAR PLEXUS; THIRD EYE
serves 2
prep time 15 MINUTES
cook time 20 MINUTES

1 Cut the tofu block into slices and spread out on several paper towels. Add more towels on top and set a cutting board or plate on top of the tofu to press. Let the tofu sit for 15 minutes to extract excess water. Then, cut the tofu into cubes.

2 Add the cornstarch to a small bowl and slowly whisk in the tamari, ensuring there are no lumps. Whisk in the sesame oil, orange juice, orange zest, honey, ginger, and garlic.

3 Heat 1 tablespoon of the avocado oil in a large skillet over medium-high heat. Add the tofu and sauté for 10 minutes, or until golden and crispy, stirring occasionally. Remove the tofu from the pan and set on paper towels to drain.

4 Heat the remaining 1 tablespoon in the pan over medium-high heat. Add the bell pepper, broccoli, and shiitake mushrooms to the pan. Season with salt and pepper and cook until the vegetables are softened but still have a slight crunch, about 6 minutes.

5 Whisk the sauce once more to incorporate and add the sauce and the tofu back to the pan. Cook until the sauce bubbles and thickens, 3 to 5 minutes. Add the toasted sesame seeds.

6 Serve the stir-fry over the base of your choice (see **customize it** below) and top with additional toasted sesame seeds, a drizzle of toasted sesame oil, and orange slices.

customize it You can also make this dish with chicken or chickpeas instead of tofu. Serve with brown rice, quinoa, or riced cauliflower.

8 ounces (225 g) extra-firm tofu

1 tablespoon cornstarch

¼ cup (60 ml) tamari

1 tablespoon toasted sesame oil, plus more for serving

½ cup (120 ml) fresh orange juice

Zest of 1 orange

1 tablespoon honey or agave

1 tablespoon freshly grated ginger

3 cloves minced garlic

2 tablespoons avocado oil

1 medium orange bell pepper, seeded and sliced

1 bunch (about 7 ounces, or 198 g) broccoli, chopped

3 ounces (85 g) shiitake mushrooms, sliced

Salt and pepper

1 tablespoon toasted sesame seeds, plus more for serving

Orange slices, for garnishing

mediterranean mezze bowls with quinoa

gluten-free · vegetarian

chakra HEART; ROOT; SOLAR PLEXUS; THIRD EYE
serves 4
prep time 20 MINUTES
cook time 20 MINUTES

One of my favorite weekly meal prep options, these Mediterranean-inspired bowls are packed with protein, fiber, healthy fats, and vitamin C. Inspired by mezze platters (appetizers consisting of several small dishes), these colorful bowls support multiple chakras while highlighting a variety of tastes and textures.

roasted garlic tomatoes

12 ounces (340 g) multicolor grape tomatoes

1 tablespoon olive oil

1 clove garlic, minced

Salt and pepper

herbed quinoa

2 tablespoons plus 1 teaspoon olive oil, divided

1 cup (170 g) quinoa, rinsed

1¾ cups (420 ml) chicken stock

½ cup (18 g) chopped fresh parsley

2 tablespoons chopped fresh mint

2 tablespoons fresh lemon juice

Salt and pepper

tzatziki

1½ cups (345 g) Greek yogurt

1 cup (100 g) grated English cucumber

2 tablespoons olive oil

2 tablespoons chopped fresh mint

1 tablespoon fresh lemon juice

1 clove garlic, grated

Salt and pepper

bowls

½ cup (75 g) mixed Greek olives, pitted

½ cup (75 g) lemon hummus

1 cup (180 g) roasted red peppers, sliced

2 cups (40 g) fresh baby spinach

8 ounces (225 g) feta, cubed

1 cucumber, cut into batons

Gluten-free pita bread triangles, for serving

1 To make the roasted tomatoes: Preheat the oven to 450°F (230°C). Line a baking sheet with parchment paper. In a large bowl, toss the tomatoes with the olive oil, garlic, salt, and pepper. Spread on the prepared baking sheet and roast for 15 minutes.

2 To make the herbed quinoa: Heat 1 teaspoon of the olive oil in a medium pot over medium-high heat. Add the quinoa and toast for 2 minutes. Pour in the stock, bring to a boil, and reduce to a simmer. Cover and cook for 15 minutes, or until the water is absorbed. Remove the pot from the heat and let it sit for 5 minutes. Fluff the quinoa with a fork and transfer it to a bowl. Add the parsley, mint, lemon juice, and remaining 2 tablespoons olive oil and toss to combine. Season with salt and pepper.

3 To make the tzatziki: In a small bowl, stir together all the ingredients until combined.

4 To make the bowls: Divide the quinoa among four bowls. To each bowl, add 2 tablespoons of olives, 2 tablespoons of lemon hummus, ¼ cup (45 g) of roasted peppers, ½ cup (10 g) of spinach, and 2 ounces (55 g) of cubed feta. Divide the cucumber and roasted tomatoes among the bowls and top with the tzatziki. Serve with pita triangles.

customize it Add your favorite protein to this dish. Tuna, grilled salmon, or roasted chicken breast pair well here.

grounding beef and mushroom stew

dairy-free · gluten-free · paleo

chakra ROOT
serves 6
prep time 20 MINUTES
cook time 4–8 HOURS

1 tablespoon olive oil

1½ pounds (680 g) boneless beef chuck, cut into 1-inch (2.5 cm) cubes

1 medium yellow onion, diced

3 cloves garlic, minced

3 medium carrots, chopped

1 medium parsnip, chopped

1½ pounds (680 g) gold or red potatoes, chopped

1 pound (455 g) cremini mushrooms, sliced

1 bay leaf

2 teaspoons dried thyme

1 teaspoon dried rosemary

2 tablespoons Worcestershire sauce or coconut aminos

2 tablespoons tomato paste

3 cups (720 ml) beef broth

Salt and pepper

2 tablespoons arrowroot powder mixed with 2 tablespoons water

Both beef and mushrooms are powerful supporters of the root chakra. Rich in earthy mushrooms and root vegetables, this slow-cooked stew offers significant amounts of fiber, vitamin A, iron, potassium, zinc, and B vitamins. This grounding recipe feeds the root chakra with an impressive 30 grams of protein per serving.

1 Heat the olive oil in a large sauté pan over medium-high heat. Working in batches if needed, add the beef chuck and cook the beef until evenly browned on all sides, about 1 minute per side. Transfer the browned beef to a slow cooker.

2 Add the onion, garlic, carrots, parsnip, potatoes, mushrooms, bay leaf, thyme, rosemary, Worcestershire sauce, tomato paste, and beef broth to the slow cooker. Stir everything together and season with salt and pepper.

3 Cook the stew on low for 8 hours or on high for 4 hours. During the last 30 minutes of cooking, add the arrowroot mixture to the stew, which will thicken the stew as it simmers.

cooking tip No slow cooker? Another great way to cook stew is in a Dutch oven, by either slowly simmering it on the stove or in a 300°F (150°C) oven. Cooking stew low and slow is crucial for tender meat.

roasted eggplant
with tahini and pomegranate

dairy-free • gluten-free • grain-free • paleo

Feed the third eye with deep purple eggplant in this Middle Eastern–inspired dish. This tender roasted eggplant is the perfect balance of sweet, savory, fruity, earthy, and nutty. A hardy plant-based staple, eggplants are abundant in antioxidant-rich anthocyanins, which provide their vibrant purple color.

1 Preheat the oven to 400°F (200°C). Line a baking sheet with parchment paper.

2 To make the eggplant: Cut the eggplants in half lengthwise, keeping the stem on. Using the tip of a knife, score the eggplant by cutting a crosshatch pattern, being careful not to cut too deep through the skin. Sprinkle the eggplants with sea salt and let sit for 10 minutes. Transfer the eggplants to the prepared baking sheet and brush both sides of the eggplants with olive oil.

3 In a small bowl, whisk together the olive oil, za'atar, and garlic. Spoon this mixture over the eggplants, rubbing the cut side of the eggplant evenly, coating the top, and pressing some of the spice mixture into the crevices. Bake the eggplant for 50 minutes, or until golden and very tender.

4 To make the tahini sauce: In a small bowl, whisk together the tahini, honey, and lemon juice. Add water, 1 tablespoon at a time, until a saucy consistency is reached. Season with salt and pepper.

5 Drizzle the eggplant with the tahini sauce and a little honey, if desired. Top with the pomegranate arils, pine nuts, and mint.

ingredient tip You can purchase za'atar or easily make the spice blend yourself. To make a simplified version, combine 1 tablespoon toasted sesame seeds, 1 tablespoon sumac, ¼ teaspoon sea salt, and 1 teaspoon dried thyme.

chakra THIRD EYE
serves 6
prep time 15 MINUTES
cook time 50 MINUTES

roasted eggplant
3 medium eggplants

Sea salt

6 tablespoons olive oil, plus more for brushing

2 tablespoons za'atar

2 cloves garlic, minced

3 tablespoons pomegranate arils, for topping

3 tablespoons toasted pine nuts, for topping

2 tablespoons chopped fresh mint, for topping

tahini sauce
¼ cup (60 ml) tahini

1 tablespoon honey, plus more for drizzling

2 tablespoons fresh lemon juice

¼ cup (60 ml) filtered water

Salt and pepper

turkey picadillo stuffed peppers

gluten-free

chakra ROOT; SOLAR PLEXUS; THIRD EYE; THROAT
serves 6
prep time 15 MINUTES
cook time 1 HOUR AND 15 MINUTES

3 tablespoons olive oil, plus more for greasing

6 large bell peppers (red, orange, and yellow), halved lengthwise and seeded

Salt and pepper

1 medium yellow onion, diced

1 medium green bell pepper, diced

3 cloves minced garlic

1 pound (455 g) ground turkey

1 tablespoon ground cumin

2 teaspoons paprika

1 teaspoon dried oregano

1 can (15 ounces, or 425 g) crushed tomatoes

½ cup (50 g) sliced pimento-stuffed green olives, plus more for serving

2 tablespoons olive brine

continued on next page

Support multiple chakras with this stuffed tricolor pepper recipe. Picadillo is a traditional Latin American dish that consists of ground beef, spices, tomatoes, olives, raisins, and almonds. It is sweet, savory, tangy, and delicious. Here, I make a protein-packed, turkey-based variation to stuff into baked bell peppers.

1 Preheat the oven to 375°F (190°C). Grease a large 16 by 11-inch (41 by 28 cm) baking dish (or two smaller ones) with oil.

2 Drizzle the pepper halves evenly with 1 tablespoon of the olive oil and season with salt and pepper. Arrange the pepper halves cut side-down in the prepared baking dish. Bake for 15 minutes. Remove from the oven and set aside.

3 Meanwhile, make the filling. In a 12-inch (30 cm) skillet, heat the remaining 2 tablespoons olive oil over medium heat. Add the onion and diced bell pepper and sauté until softened and golden, 6 to 8 minutes. Stir in the garlic and cook until fragrant, 1 minute more.

4 Move the vegetables to the sides of the skillet to create room in the middle of the pan. Add the ground turkey. Let it brown on one side, crumble it with a wooden spoon, and cook until no longer pink, 5 to 6 minutes. Season with salt and pepper and stir in the cumin, paprika, and oregano. Cook for 1 minute and stir in the crushed tomatoes.

5 Reduce the heat to medium-low and simmer the turkey mixture for 8 minutes, stirring occasionally. Stir in the olives, olive brine, raisins, and almonds. Cook for another 5 minutes, or until the sauce is thickened. Stir in the brown rice and remove from the heat. Season the mixture with more salt or pepper, if needed.

6 Flip the peppers over and stuff the peppers with the turkey filling. The filling should be jammy and stuff easily. Using the back of a spoon, pack the filling into all crevices of the pepper and fill with a slight mound on top.

7 Sprinkle each pepper with 2 tablespoons of the shredded cheese. Loosely cover the baking dish with foil and bake for 20 minutes. Then, uncover and bake for 15 minutes more, until the cheese is lightly browned.

8 Serve the peppers garnished with chopped cilantro and additional chopped olives.

customize it Make this recipe plant-based by swapping the ground turkey for textured vegetable protein or cooked lentils.

¼ cup (35 g) Thompson raisins

¼ cup (25 g) chopped roasted almonds

1 cup (200 g) cooked medium-grain brown rice

1½ cups (170 g) shredded mozzarella

Chopped cilantro, for serving

hearty
vegetarian chili

dairy-free • **gluten-free** • **one pan** • **vegan**

chakra ROOT; SOLAR PLEXUS; THIRD EYE
serves 6
prep time 15 MINUTES
cook time 45 MINUTES

2 tablespoons olive oil

1 medium yellow onion, diced

1 medium red bell pepper, seeded and diced

1 large carrot, diced

1 large sweet potato, peeled and diced

1 jalapeño, seeded and diced

3 cloves garlic, minced

Salt and pepper

1 tablespoon chili powder

2 teaspoons ground cumin

1 teaspoon dried oregano

2 teaspoons unsweetened cacao powder

1 bay leaf

1 can (28 ounces, or 793 g) fire-roasted diced tomatoes

1 cup (135 g) frozen corn

1 cup (240 ml) vegetable broth

1 can (15 ounces, or 425 g) red kidney beans, rinsed and drained

1 can (15 ounces, or 425 g) pinto beans, rinsed and drained

Fiber-rich vegetarian chilis are a great way to get a generous serving of plant-based protein. This chili contains warming spices, plenty of veggies, and heart-healthy beans. Studies have found that just one serving of beans or legumes daily is associated with a 38 percent lower risk of heart attack.

1 Heat the olive oil in a large pot or Dutch oven over medium heat. Add the onion and cook for about 5 minutes, or until softened and translucent.

2 Stir in the bell pepper, carrot, sweet potato, jalapeño, and garlic. Season with salt and pepper and cook for another 5 minutes. Stir in the chili powder, cumin, oregano, cacao powder, and bay leaf. Stir to coat the vegetables in the spices and cook until fragrant, about 2 minutes.

3 Stir in the diced tomatoes (with their juices), corn, vegetable broth, kidney beans, and pinto beans. Bring to a simmer.

4 Once simmering, lower the heat to medium-low and partially cover. Cook the chili for 30 minutes, stirring occasionally. Taste and adjust the seasonings and salt as necessary. Remove the bay leaf before serving.

serving tip Serve this chili with lime wedges, shredded Cheddar, sliced avocado, pickled onions, Greek yogurt, and/or chopped cilantro.

customize it Want it spicy? Keep a few jalapeño seeds for extra heat or top with jalapeño slices. Like a looser chili? Add up to another 1 cup (240 ml) of vegetable broth.

soul-warming
kitchari

dairy-free · gluten-free · one pan · vegan

Kitchari—a nourishing porridge-like dish consisting of rice, mung beans, and spices—is a traditional Ayurvedic recipe that is easy to digest and typically used for cleansing. High in fiber and protein, this porridge especially feeds the solar plexus with an intense yellow hue and warming spices.

chakra SOLAR PLEXUS; THIRD EYE; THROAT
serves 4
prep time 15 MINUTES
cook time 40 MINUTES

1 cup (195 g) yellow split mung beans

½ cup (85 g) basmati rice

1 tablespoon ghee or coconut oil

1 teaspoon mustard seeds

1 teaspoon fennel seeds

1 teaspoon cumin seeds

1 clove garlic, minced

1 piece (1-inch, or 2.5 cm) ginger, peeled and grated

1 teaspoon ground cumin

1 bay leaf

1 teaspoon coriander

1 teaspoon turmeric

1 large carrot, diced

1 head (7 ounces, or 198 g) broccoli, finely chopped

3 cups (720 ml) water

2 cups (480 ml) vegetable broth

Salt and pepper

1 packed cup (20 g) baby spinach, chopped

1 In a medium bowl, combine the beans and rice. Pour enough water to cover the mixture and soak for 15 minutes. Strain through a fine-mesh strainer and rinse with cold water until it runs clear. Set aside.

2 Heat the ghee in a Dutch oven or large stockpot over medium heat. Once hot, add the mustard seeds, fennel seeds, and cumin seeds. Sauté for 1 minute until fragrant, then stir in the garlic, ginger, ground cumin, bay leaf, coriander, and turmeric. Sauté for another minute.

3 Add the beans and rice to the stockpot and stir to coat in the spices. Stir in the carrot, broccoli, water, and vegetable broth. Season with salt and pepper and bring to a simmer.

4 Reduce the heat to medium-low and cover. Cook the kitchari until it is soft and creamy with a porridge-like texture, about 30 minutes. Stir in the chopped spinach during the last 5 minutes of cooking. Taste and adjust the seasoning and add more salt as needed.

serving tip Spruce up this dish with toppings like chopped cilantro, lime wedges, Greek yogurt, or chili flakes.

ingredient tip Yellow split mung beans are also commonly referred to as moong dal. You can find these in the international or Indian food aisles at most grocery stores or online.

Roasted Sweet Potato
Hummus

snacks & treats

pink pitaya coconut truffles

dairy-free · gluten-free · grain-free · vegan

chakra HEART; SACRAL
makes 12
prep time 20 MINUTES
inactive prep time
1 HOUR AND 10 MINUTES

1 cup (70 g)
desiccated coconut

1 tablespoon
pink pitaya powder

1 tablespoon plus
1 teaspoon coconut oil,
melted, divided

1 tablespoon maple syrup

1½ tablespoons
coconut cream

½ teaspoon vanilla extract

Pinch of salt

½ cup (85 g) finely
chopped semisweet or
dark chocolate

Dried rose petals
(optional)

ingredient tip Pink pitaya
powder can be easily
ordered online. Several
retailers such as Suncore
Foods specialize in making
vibrant and colorful fruit
and vegetable powders.

Feed your heart with pretty pink pitaya truffles. These antioxidant-rich vegan truffles combine pitaya powder with coconut and chocolate for a sweet treat that's just as lovely to look at as it is to eat.

1 In a medium bowl, stir together the desiccated coconut and pitaya powder until the coconut is evenly coated and turns pink.

2 In a small bowl, whisk together 1 tablespoon of the melted coconut oil, maple syrup, coconut cream, vanilla, and a pinch of salt. Pour this mixture over the coconut and stir together until everything is moistened and evenly combined.

3 Refrigerate the mixture for 1 hour, or until it is firm enough to form balls. Line a small baking sheet with parchment paper. Form the mixture into 12 balls and transfer to the prepared baking sheet. Freeze the balls until very firm, about 10 minutes.

4 In a microwave-safe bowl, melt the chocolate and remaining 1 teaspoon coconut oil in the microwave at 50 percent power, microwaving for 15-second intervals and stirring in between, until smooth and evenly melted.

5 Using a fork, dip each truffle into the melted chocolate and then spoon chocolate over the top. Lift the truffle up and tap the fork against the bowl gently so excess chocolate falls through the fork tines.

6 Refrigerate the truffles until set. Drizzle with additional melted chocolate and top with a few dried rose petals, if desired.

storage tip These truffles will keep in an airtight container for up to 3 days in the refrigerator, but will taste best fresh.

matcha frozen yogurt bark

gluten-free · grain-free · vegetarian

Since returning from a recent trip to Japan, I have found myself sneaking matcha into anything and everything I can. Matcha is packed with antioxidants and L-theanine, an amino acid that has been shown to improve anxiety, mood, and cognitive function when paired with caffeine. Here, earthy matcha perfectly pairs with honey, raspberries, and coconut to create a cooling, tasty treat.

1 To make the frozen yogurt bark: Line a 12 by 17-inch (30 by 43 cm) baking sheet with parchment or wax paper.

2 In a medium mixing bowl, whisk the yogurt until smooth. Whisk in the vanilla and honey. Finally, whisk in the matcha powder until smooth and combined with no lumps of powder.

3 Spread the yogurt mixture evenly on the prepared pan using an offset spatula. Sprinkle the freeze-dried raspberries on top of the yogurt, lightly crushing the larger pieces, followed by the coconut flakes. Freeze the yogurt until set, about 3 hours.

4 To make the matcha glaze (if using): In a small microwave-safe bowl, melt the white chocolate in the microwave at 50 percent power in 20-second intervals, stirring in between, until evenly smooth. Stir in the matcha and drizzle the yogurt bark with the glaze once frozen.

5 Once frozen, cut the bark into roughly 15 pieces. Store in an airtight glass container with wax or parchment paper between each layer.

chakra HEART; ROOT; SOLAR PLEXUS
serves 15
prep time 10 MINUTES
inactive prep time 3 HOURS

frozen yogurt bark

2 cups (460 g) whole milk plain Greek yogurt

1 teaspoon vanilla extract

3 tablespoons honey

2 tablespoons plus 1 teaspoon matcha powder, divided

½ cup (60 g) freeze-dried raspberries

¼ cup (20 g) unsweetened coconut flakes

matcha glaze (optional)

2 ounces (55 g) white chocolate, preferably no sugar added

1 teaspoon matcha powder

ingredient tip Using full-fat yogurt ensures that your bark is as creamy as possible. You can use a lower-fat yogurt, but your bark may be icier due to the higher water content.

adaptogenic energy bites

dairy-free · gluten-free · quick & easy · vegan

chakra SACRAL;
SOLAR PLEXUS; THIRD EYE
makes 12
prep time 15 MINUTES

¾ cup (65 g) rolled oats

2 tablespoons
chocolate protein powder

1 tablespoon chia seeds

Pinch of salt

½ cup (120 ml) creamy
almond butter

⅓ cup (80 ml) maple syrup

½ teaspoon vanilla extract

½ teaspoon
ground cinnamon

1 teaspoon
ashwagandha powder

1 teaspoon maca powder

¼ cup (45 g)
mini dark chocolate chips

The perfect portable pick-me-up or two-bite snack, these small but mighty energy bites are packed with nutrients and fuel. This version includes ashwagandha and maca, powerful adaptogens that help the body manage stress and aid in sleep, brain, and sexual health.

1 In a medium bowl, stir together the oats, protein powder, chia seeds, and salt.

2 In a medium to large bowl, whisk together the almond butter, maple syrup, and vanilla. Whisk in the cinnamon, ashwagandha, and maca until the mixture is smooth with no lumps.

3 Add the oat mixture to the wet mixture and stir until combined. Stir in the chocolate chips. (You may find it easier to use your hands for this step.)

4 Roll the mixture into 12 balls. Place in the refrigerator until firm and store in an airtight container in the fridge.

cooking tip Since all nut butters vary in thickness, you may need to adjust the texture of your energy bites. If your mixture is too dry, add water or nut milk 1 tablespoon at a time until your desired texture is reached. The mixture should be sticky but hold its shape when rolled into balls.

roasted sweet potato hummus

dairy-free · gluten-free · grain-free · vegan

Besides feeding the sacral chakra, this orange-hued hummus supports the heart and solar plexus chakras with warming spices, complex carbs, and heart-healthy ingredients. This snack is packed with protein, fiber, and vitamins C and A. Serve with pita chips or your favorite crisp veggies.

1 Preheat the oven to 425°F (220°C). Line a baking sheet with parchment paper.

2 In a large bowl, add the cubed sweet potato and garlic and drizzle with 1 tablespoon of the olive oil. Season with salt and pepper. Transfer to the prepared baking sheet and bake for 25 minutes, or until golden brown and tender. Let cool.

3 Add the sweet potatoes and garlic to a food processor. Add the chickpeas, lemon juice, tahini, cumin, turmeric, salt, pepper, and 3 remaining tablespoons olive oil. Process until completely blended and smooth. Add the cold water, little by little, until a very creamy consistency is reached.

4 Serve with additional olive oil drizzled on top, sesame seeds, and chopped parsley.

customize it If you follow a paleo diet or do not eat legumes, you can make a sweet potato "hummus" without chickpeas. Simply substitute the chickpeas in this recipe with an additional sweet potato, use 2 tablespoons of olive oil when roasting (and 2 tablespoons when blending), and skip the water at the end.

chakra HEART; SACRAL; SOLAR PLEXUS
serves 6–8
prep time 10 MINUTES
cook time 25 MINUTES

1 small to medium sweet potato, peeled and cubed

3 cloves garlic, smashed

4 tablespoons olive oil, divided, plus more for drizzling

Salt and pepper

1 can chickpeas (15 ounces, or 425 g), rinsed and drained

Juice of 1 lemon (2 to 3 tablespoons)

¼ cup (60 ml) tahini

1 teaspoon ground cumin

½ teaspoon ground turmeric

½ cup (120 ml) cold filtered water, as needed

Toasted sesame seeds, for serving

Finely chopped parsley, for serving

chakra charcuterie

Feed the chakras by making a vibrant charcuterie board that showcases all the colors of the rainbow. This beautiful board is great for crowds or special occasions, but you can also pick and choose items to make smaller platters or snack plates. Take inspiration from these foods and don't be afraid to create your own combinations!

chakra HEART; ROOT; SACRAL; SOLAR PLEXUS; THIRD EYE; THROAT
serves VARIES
prep time 35 MINUTES

red items
Raspberries

Prosciutto roses

Tomato bruschetta

Red bell pepper strips

Grape or sun-dried tomatoes

orange items
Carrot sticks

Dried apricots

Orange bell pepper strips

Sliced sharp Cheddar cheese

Roasted Sweet Potato Hummus (page 169)

yellow items
Pita chips

Crackers

Pineapple slices

Yellow bell pepper strips

Yellow cauliflower florets

green items
Snap peas

Pistachios

Green grapes

Guacamole

Broccoli florets

Cucumber sticks

Castelvetrano olives

blue items
Blueberries

Blackberries

Dried or fresh figs

Chunk of blue cheese

Blueberry goat cheese log

purple items
Purple grapes

Olive tapenade

Purple carrot sticks

Purple cauliflower

Baked Beet Chips (page 179) or store-bought beet or purple sweet potato chips

Chocolate-Dipped Stuffed Dates (page 175) with lavender buds

Assemble and arrange all items by color groups on a large board or platter.

salted honey
and maca fudge

dairy-free · gluten-free · grain-free · paleo · vegetarian

chakra SACRAL;
THIRD EYE; THROAT
makes 20
prep time 10 MINUTES
inactive prep time
2 HOURS

1 cup (240 ml)
creamy almond butter

¼ cup (60 ml) honey

½ cup (120 ml)
coconut oil, melted

¼ cup (25 g)
raw cacao powder

2 tablespoons
powdered maca

Pink Himalayan sea salt,
for sprinkling

"Freezer fudge" is a quick and easy way to make a rich, satisfying treat. This third eye powerhouse highlights maca, a nutrient-packed adaptogen that has been shown to promote fertility and sexual function, improve energy, and enhance brain health.

1 In a medium bowl, whisk together the almond butter and honey until combined. Whisk in the coconut oil, little by little, until smooth. Finally, whisk in the cacao powder and maca until smooth with no lumps.

2 Pour the mixture into a plastic-lined square or rectangular container (8 by 6 inches, or 20 by 15 cm, or similar) or into individual silicone molds. Freeze until solid, about 2 hours.

3 Unmold the fudge if using silicone molds or flip over, remove the plastic, and cut into 20 squares if using a container. Sprinkle the fudge with pink sea salt.

storage tip This fudge needs to be kept in the freezer. Store the fudge in an airtight container in the freezer for up to 2 months. Let the fudge squares sit at room temperature for a few minutes to soften slightly before eating.

customize it Swap the honey for agave or maple syrup to make this fudge vegan.

chocolate-dipped stuffed dates

dairy-free ⋅ gluten-free ⋅ grain-free ⋅ quick & easy ⋅ vegan

Rich, sweet, and chewy, these chocolate-dipped dates are one of my favorite snacks. Stuffed with creamy almond butter and a whole almond for crunch, each of these dates is enveloped in dark chocolate for a decadent treat. Medjool dates are high in antioxidants and have been shown to help boost brain health.

chakra SACRAL; THIRD EYE
makes 20
prep time 30 MINUTES

20 fresh, pitted Medjool dates

6 tablespoons creamy almond butter

20 whole roasted almonds

1 cup (170 g) finely chopped dark chocolate

2 teaspoons coconut oil

topping ideas
flaky sea salt, candied orange peel, shredded coconut, crushed freeze-dried strawberries, chopped pistachios, chopped almonds, crushed dried rose petals, or dried lavender sprigs

1 Using a small, sharp knife, make a slit in each date, being careful not to cut all the way through. Stuff the dates with the almond butter. Depending on the size of your dates, this will be ½ to 1 teaspoon of almond butter.

2 Gently press a whole almond into the center and close the date slightly to seal. Place the dates on a baking sheet and freeze for 15 minutes.

3 Place the chocolate and coconut oil in a small microwave-safe bowl. Melt the chocolate and oil in the microwave at 50 percent power, microwaving for 15-second intervals and stirring in between, until smooth and evenly melted.

4 Line a baking sheet with parchment paper. Using a fork, dip each date into the melted chocolate and then spoon chocolate over the top. Lift the date up and tap the fork against the glass bowl gently, so excess chocolate falls through the fork tines. Transfer to the baking sheet.

5 Sprinkle with or roll in your desired toppings before the chocolate sets. Refrigerate until set.

storage tip Store dates in an airtight container in the refrigerator for up to 1 week or freeze for up to 3 months.

summer fruit salad
with ginger-lime dressing

dairy-free · gluten-free · grain-free · quick & easy · vegetarian

chakra HEART;
ROOT; THROAT
serves 8
prep time 15 MINUTES

dressing
2 tablespoons honey

2 tablespoons agave

2 tablespoons fresh
lime juice

1 teaspoon lime zest

1 teaspoon
grated fresh ginger

fruit salad
2 cups (300 g) cubed
seedless watermelon

1½ cups (235 g)
red cherries,
pitted and halved

2 medium peaches
or nectarines,
pitted and sliced

3 medium apricots,
pitted and sliced

1½ cups (225 g)
strawberries, halved

1½ cups (210 g)
blackberries

2 medium oranges,
peeled and segmented

Fresh mint, for garnishing

Loaded with fiber and vitamin C, this fruit salad is a wonderful way to enjoy seasonal summer produce and stone fruits while supporting the root, heart, and throat chakras. A honeyed dressing with fresh lime and ginger makes this a refreshing and sweet treat.

1 To make the dressing: Combine all the ingredients in a small bowl. Let the dressing sit and allow the flavors to meld while preparing the fruit.

2 To make the fruit salad: Add the watermelon, cherries, peaches, apricots, strawberries, blackberries, and oranges to a large bowl. Pour the dressing over the fruit and very gently toss. Transfer to a serving platter or bowl and garnish with fresh mint.

customize it You can use any combination of your favorite fruits to make this versatile salad. To make this recipe vegan, use all agave and skip the honey.

baked beet chips
with labneh za'atar dip

gluten-free · vegetarian

When it comes to veggie chips, beets may be my favorite—especially when paired with a creamy za'atar-spiced labneh dip.

chakra ROOT; SOLAR PLEXUS; THIRD EYE
serves 6
prep time 20 MINUTES
cook time 30 MINUTES

2 large red beets

Salt and pepper

Olive oil spray

1 cup (230 g) labneh

1 clove grated garlic

2 teaspoons lemon juice

1 tablespoon olive oil

2 teaspoons za'atar

1 to 2 tablespoons pomegranate arils

1 tablespoon chopped fresh parsley or mint

1 Preheat the oven to 300°F (150°C), and line two 21 by 15-inch (53 by 38 cm) baking pans with parchment paper.

2 Scrub the beets very well under cold water. Leaving the skins on, slice the beets with a mandoline into paper-thin 1/16-inch (1.5 mm) slices.

3 In a large bowl, toss the beets with a generous seasoning of salt. Let the beets sit in this salt mixture for 20 minutes to release their juices.

4 After 20 minutes, drain the liquid and pat the beets dry with paper towels. Spray the prepared pans with olive oil. Arrange the beets on the pans in an even layer. Do not overlap the beets. Spray the tops of the beets lightly with olive oil.

5 Bake the beet chips for 15 minutes, then remove and flip them over. Return them to the oven and bake for an additional 15 to 30 minutes, or until crispy and wrinkled at the edges. Watch closely as the time will vary depending on the size of the chips.

6 Remove the pans from the oven and transfer the beet chips to a cooling rack (optional, but doing so will create crispier chips). While they are still warm, sprinkle more salt to taste, if desired.

7 In a medium or shallow bowl, mix together the labneh and garlic and season with salt and pepper. Whisk in the lemon juice and whip the mixture until creamy. Smooth out the labneh so it's in a shallow layer. Drizzle with the olive oil and sprinkle with the za'atar. Top with the pomegranate arils and parsley. Serve the dip with the beet chips.

ingredient tip For a visually stunning dish, you can use a variety of colored beets such as red, golden, and candy-striped.

strawberry rhubarb crisp

dairy-free · gluten-free · vegetarian

chakra ROOT;
SOLAR PLEXUS; THIRD EYE
serves 8
prep time 15 MINUTES
cook time 40 MINUTES

This ruby red crisp feeds the root chakra with fresh strawberries and tart rhubarb. Dairy-free and gluten-free, this dessert uses honey and coconut as sweeteners and coconut oil and oats to make a crisp topping.

1½ pounds (682 g) strawberries, halved

2 cups (162 g) rhubarb, sliced

1 teaspoon vanilla extract

2 tablespoons fresh orange juice

2 tablespoons arrowroot powder

⅓ cup (80 ml) honey

1 cup (90 g) rolled oats

¾ cup (85 g) almond flour

½ cup (95 g) coconut sugar

¼ teaspoon salt

½ teaspoon ground cinnamon

6 tablespoons coconut oil, melted

Ice cream, frozen yogurt, or whipped coconut cream, for serving (optional)

1 Preheat the oven to 350°F (180°C).

2 In a large bowl, toss the strawberries and rhubarb with the vanilla and orange juice. Sprinkle with the arrowroot powder and then fold in until dissolved. Gently stir in the honey until combined and transfer to a 9 by 9-inch (23 by 23 cm) baking pan (or similar size).

3 In a large bowl, mix together the oats, almond flour, coconut sugar, salt, and cinnamon until combined. Stir in the melted coconut oil until everything is moistened and clumps form, using your hands or a wooden spoon.

4 Using your hands, press some of the mixture together to form a clump and then gently break it over the fruit filling. Repeat this until all of the mixture is evenly covering the fruit.

5 Bake for 40 minutes, or until the topping is golden brown and the filling is bubbling. Let sit at room temperature for 10 minutes to cool slightly. Serve with ice cream if desired.

customize it If you want your crisp to have more of a citrusy punch, grate some orange zest (about 1 teaspoon) before juicing your orange and mix it into the oat topping. Cornstarch can also be used in place of arrowroot as a thickening agent.

acknowledgments

A special thank you to Michelle Miller, Sara Grohsman, and Sarah Drake.

about the author

Tiffany La Forge is a professional chef, food blogger, writer, and certified chakra energy healer. Her love for cooking has always been a constant in her life. She is a graduate of the Institute of Culinary Education in New York City. In addition to her work in the culinary field, she runs the popular blog *Parsnips and Pastries* (parsnipsandpastries.com). Her blog showcases a collection of seasonal, balanced, and approachable recipes.

She has a passion for using food and nutrition to boost overall wellness, improve mental health, and support the mind-body connection. For the past decade, she has been a regular columnist for notable publications such as *Healthline*, *Greatist*, and Sleep.com, where her pieces focus on holistic well-being.

Tiffany lives in Maui, Hawaii, with her husband, Ryan, and two dogs, Cocoa and Kona. She is a passionate advocate for mental health and women's empowerment.

Find her on Instagram @parsnipsandpastries.

references

Abbasi, B., Kimiagar, M., Sadeghniiat, K., Shirazi, M. M., Hedayati, M., & Rashidkhani, B. (2012). "The Effect of Magnesium Supplementation on Primary Insomnia in Elderly: A Double-Blind Placebo-Controlled Clinical Trial." *Journal of Research in Medical Sciences: The Official Journal of Isfahan University of Medical Sciences,* *17*(12), 1161–1169.

Agagündüz, D., Sahin, T. Ö., Yılmaz, B., Ekenci, K. D., Duyar Özer, S., & Capasso, R. (2022). "Cruciferous Vegetables and Their Bioactive Metabolites: from Prevention to Novel Therapies of Colorectal Cancer." *Evidence-Based Complementary and Alternative Medicine: eCAM,* 2022, 1534083. https://doi.org/10.1155/2022/1534083.

Alberts, B., Johnson, A., Lewis, J., et al. (2002). *Molecular Biology of the Cell.* 4th edition. New York: Garland Science. "Protein Function." https://www.ncbi.nlm.nih.gov/books/NBK26911/.

Bird, R. J., Hoggard, N., & Aceves-Martins, M. (2022). "The Effect of Grape Interventions on Cognitive and Mental Performance in Healthy Participants and Those with Mild Cognitive Impairment: A Systematic Review of Randomized Controlled Trials." *Nutrition Reviews,* *80*(3), 367–380. https://doi.org/10.1093/nutrit/nuab025.

Brookie, K. L., Best, G. I., & Conner, T. S. (2018). "Intake of Raw Fruits and Vegetables Is Associated With Better Mental Health Than Intake of Processed Fruits and Vegetables." *Frontiers in Psychology,* *9,* 487. https://doi.org/10.3389/fpsyg.2018.00487.

Carlson, J. L., Erickson, J. M., Lloyd, B. B., & Slavin, J. L. (2018). "Health Effects and Sources of Prebiotic Dietary Fiber." *Current Developments in Nutrition,* *2*(3), nzy005. https://doi.org/10.1093/cdn/nzy005.

Crichton, G. E., Elias, M. F., & Alkerwi, A. (2016). "Chocolate Intake is Associated with Better Cognitive Function: The Maine-Syracuse Longitudinal Study." *Appetite,* *100,* 126–132. https://doi.org/10.1016/j.appet.2016.02.010.

Dietz, C., & Dekker, M. (2017). "Effect of Green Tea Phytochemicals on Mood and Cognition." *Current Pharmaceutical Design,* *23*(19), 2876–2905. https://doi.org/10.2174/1381612823666170105151800.

Eugene, A. R., & Masiak, J. (2015). "The Neuroprotective Aspects of Sleep." *MEDtube Science,* *3*(1), 35–40.

Finicelli, M., Di Salle, A., Galderisi, U., & Peluso, G. (2022). "The Mediterranean Diet: An Update of the Clinical Trials." *Nutrients,* *14*(14), 2956. https://doi.org/10.3390/nu14142956.

Grune, T., Lietz, G., Palou, A., Ross, A. C., Stahl, W., Tang, G., Thurnham, D., Yin, S. A., & Biesalski, H. K. (2010). "Beta-Carotene Is an Important Vitamin A Source for Humans." *The Journal of Nutrition,* *140*(12), 2268S–2285S. https://doi.org/10.3945/jn.109.119024.

Hein, S., Whyte, A. R., Wood, E., Rodriguez-Mateos, A., & Williams, C. M. (2019). "Systematic Review of the Effects of Blueberry on Cognitive Performance as We Age." *The Journals of Gerontology. Series A, Biological Sciences and Medical Sciences,* *74*(7), 984–995. https://doi.org/10.1093/gerona/glz082.

Holesh, J. E., Aslam, S., & Martin, A. (2023). "Physiology, Carbohydrates." In *StatPearls* [Internet]. Treasure Island (FL): StatPearls Publishing. https://www.ncbi.nlm.nih.gov/books/NBK459280/.

Hunt, V. V. (1986, January 25). Bioenergy Field Foundation: Auric Field Demo [Video].

Imran, M., Ghorat, F., Ul-Haq, I., Ur-Rehman, H., Aslam, F., Heydari, M., Shariati, M. A., Okuskhanova, E., Yessimbekov, Z., Thiruvengadam, M., Hashempur, M. H., & Rebezov, M. (2020). "Lycopene as a Natural Antioxidant Used to Prevent Human Health Disorders." *Antioxidants (Basel, Switzerland)* , *9* (8), 706. https://doi.org/10.3390/antiox9080706.

Kechagia, M., Basoulis, D., Konstantopoulou, S., Dimitriadi, D., Gyftopoulou, K., Skarmoutsou, N., & Fakiri, E. M. (2013). "Health Benefits of Probiotics: A Review." *ISRN Nutrition*, 2013, 481651. https://doi.org/10.5402/2013/481651.

Kelly, E., Vyas, P., & Weber, J. T. (2017). "Biochemical Properties and Neuroprotective Effects of Compounds in Various Species of Berries." *Molecules (Basel, Switzerland)*, *23*(1), 26. https://doi.org/10.3390/molecules23010026

Khoo, H. E., Azlan, A., Tang, S. T., & Lim, S. M. (2017). "Anthocyanidins and Anthocyanins: Colored Pigments as Food, Pharmaceutical Ingredients, and the Potential Health Benefits." *Food & Nutrition Research*, *61* (1), 1361779. https://doi.org/10.1080/16546628.2017.1361779.

Kiecolt-Glaser, J. K., Belury, M. A., Andridge, R., Malarkey, W. B., & Glaser, R. (2011). "Omega-3 Supplementation Lowers Inflammation and Anxiety in Medical Students: A Randomized Controlled Trial." *Brain, Behavior, and Immunity*, *25*(8), 1725–1734. https://doi.org/10.1016/j.bbi.2011.07.229.

Knez, E., Kadac-Czapska, K., Dmochowska-Slezak, K., & Grembecka, M. (2022). "Root Vegetables-Composition, Health Effects, and Contaminants." *International Journal of Environmental Research and Public Health*, *19*(23), 15531. https://doi.org/10.3390/ijerph192315531.

Komada, Y., Okajima, I., & Kuwata, T. (2020). "The Effects of Milk and Dairy Products on Sleep: A Systematic Review." *International Journal of Environmental Research and Public Health*, *17*(24), 9440. https://doi.org/10.3390/ijerph17249440.

Kotta, S., Ansari, S. H., & Ali, J. (2013). "Exploring Scientifically Proven Herbal Aphrodisiacs." *Pharmacognosy Reviews*, *7*(13), 1–10. https://doi.org/10.4103/0973-7847.112832.

Kupcova, I., Danisovic, L., Klein, M., & Harsanyi, S. (2023). "Effects of the COVID-19 Pandemic on Mental Health, Anxiety, and Depression." *BMC Psychology*, *11*(1), 108. https://doi.org/10.1186/s40359-023-01130-5.

Liao, L. Y., He, Y. F., Li, L., Meng, H., Dong, Y. M., Yi, F., & Xiao, P. G. (2018). "A Preliminary Review of Studies on Adaptogens: Comparison of Their Bioactivity in TCM with That of Ginseng-Like Herbs Used Worldwide." *Chinese Medicine*, *13*, 57. https://doi.org/10.1186/s13020-018-0214-9.

Losso, J. N., Finley, J. W., Karki, N., Liu, A. G., Prudente, A., Tipton, R., Yu, Y., & Greenway, F. L. (2018). "Pilot Study of the Tart Cherry Juice for the Treatment of Insomnia and Investigation of Mechanisms." *American Journal of Therapeutics*, *25*(2), e194–e201. https://doi.org/10.1097/MJT.0000000000000584.

Mandal, M. D., & Mandal, S. (2011). "Honey: Its Medicinal Property and Antibacterial Activity." *Asian Pacific Journal of Tropical Biomedicine*, *1*(2), 154–160. https://doi.org/10.1016/S2221-1691(11)60016-6.

Mazaheri Nia, L., Iravani, M., Abedi, P., & Cheraghian, B. (2021). "Effect of Zinc on Testosterone Levels and Sexual Function of Postmenopausal Women: A Randomized Controlled Trial." *Journal of Sex & Marital Therapy*, *47*(8), 804–813. https://doi.org/10.1080/0092623X.2021.1957732.

McRae, M. P. (2017). "Health Benefits of Dietary Whole Grains: An Umbrella Review of Meta-Analyses." *Journal of Chiropractic Medicine*, *16*(1), 10–18. https://doi.org/10.1016/j.jcm.2016.08.008.

Minich, D. M. (2019). "A Review of the Science of Colorful, Plant-Based Food and Practical Strategies for 'Eating the Rainbow'." *Journal of Nutrition and Metabolism*, 2125070. https://doi.org/10.1155/2019/2125070.

Ormsby, S. M. (2021). "Hot and Cold Theory: Evidence in Nutrition." *Advances in Experimental Medicine and Biology*, *1343*, 87–107. https://doi.org/10.1007/978-3-030-80983-6_6.

Oschman, J. L., Chevalier, G., & Brown, R. (2015). "The Effects of Grounding (Earthing) on Inflammation, the Immune Response, Wound Healing, and Prevention and Treatment of Chronic Inflammatory and Autoimmune Diseases." *Journal of Inflammation Research*, *8*, 83–96. https://doi.org/10.2147/JIR.S69656

Poulose, S. M., Fisher, D. R., Larson, J., Bielinski, D. F., Rimando, A. M., Carey, A. N., Schauss, A. G., & Shukitt-Hale, B. (2012). "Anthocyanin-Rich Açai (*Euterpe oleracea Mart.*) Fruit Pulp Fractions Attenuate Inflammatory Stress Signaling in Mouse Brain BV-2 Microglial Cells." *Journal of Agricultural and Food Chemistry, 60*(4), 1084–1093. https://doi.org/10.1021/jf203989k

Sadeghi, N., Paknezhad, F., Rashidi Nooshabadi, M., Kavianpour, M., Jafari Rad, S., & Khadem Haghighian, H. (2018). "Vitamin E and Fish Oil, Separately or in Combination, on Treatment of Primary Dysmenorrhea: A Double-Blind, Randomized Clinical Trial." *Gynecological Endocrinology, 34*(9), 804-808. DOI: 10.1080/09513590.2018.1450377.

Shi, L. H., Balakrishnan, K., Thiagarajah, K., Mohd Ismail, N. I., & Yin, O. S. (2016). "Beneficial Properties of Probiotics." *Tropical Life Sciences Research, 27*(2), 73–90. https://doi.org/10.21315/tlsr2016.27.2.6.

Silva, T., Jesus, M., Cagigal, C., & Silva, C. (2019). "Food with Influence in the Sexual and Reproductive Health." *Current Pharmaceutical Biotechnology, 20*(2), 114–122. https://doi.org/10.2174/1389201019666180925140400

St-Onge, M. P., Mikic, A., & Pietrolungo, C. E. (2016). "Effects of Diet on Sleep Quality." *Advances in Nutrition, 7*(5), 938–949. https://doi.org/10.3945/an.116.012336.

Surette, M. E. (2008). "The Science Behind Dietary Omega-3 Fatty Acids." *CMAJ: Canadian Medical Association Journal, 178*(2), 177–180. https://doi.org/10.1503/cmaj.071356.

Wallace, C. J. K., & Milev, R. (2017). "The Effects of Probiotics on Depressive Symptoms in Humans: A Systematic Review." *Annals of General Psychiatry, 16*, 14. https://doi.org/10.1186/s12991-017-0138-2.

Wang, E., & Wink, M. (2016). "Chlorophyll Enhances Oxidative Stress Tolerance in *Caenorhabditis elegans* and Extends Its Lifespan." *PeerJ, 4*, e1879. https://doi.org/10.7717/peerj.1879.

Wang, R., Paul, V. J., & Luesch, H. (2013). "Seaweed Extracts and Unsaturated Fatty Acid Constituents from the Green Alga *Ulva lactuca* as Activators of the Cytoprotective Nrf2-ARE Pathway." *Free Radical Biology & Medicine, 57*, 141–153. https://doi.org/10.1016/j.freeradbiomed.2012.12.019.

Wells, M. L., Potin, P., Craigie, J. S., Raven, J. A., Merchant, S. S., Helliwell, K. E., Smith, A. G., Camire, M. E., & Brawley, S. H. (2017). "Algae as Nutritional and Functional Food Sources: Revisiting Our Understanding." *Journal of Applied Phycology, 29*(2), 949–982. https://doi.org/10.1007/s10811-016-0974-5.

Wood, A. M., Maltby, J., Gillett, R., Linley, P. A., & Joseph, S. (2008). "The Role of Gratitude in the Development of Social Support, Stress, and Depression: Two Longitudinal Studies." *Journal of Research in Personality, 42*(4), 854-871. ISSN 0092-6566. doi:10.1016/j.jrp.2007.11.003.

Zamir, A., Ben-Zeev, T., & Hoffman, J. R. (2021). "Manipulation of Dietary Intake on Changes in Circulating Testosterone Concentrations." *Nutrients, 13*(10), 3375. https://doi.org/10.3390/nu13103375.

Zurbau, A., Au-Yeung, F., Blanco Mejia, S., Khan, T. A., Vuksan, V., Jovanovski, E., Leiter, L. A., Kendall, C. W. C., Jenkins, D. J. A., & Sievenpiper, J. L. (2020). "Relation of Different Fruit and Vegetable Sources With Incident Cardiovascular Outcomes: A Systematic Review and Meta-Analysis of Prospective Cohort Studies." *Journal of the American Heart Association, 9*, e017728. doi:10.1161/JAHA.120.017728.

index of recipes by chakra

root chakra

sacral chakra

solar plexus chakra

index

First published in 2024 by Wellfleet Press,
an imprint of The Quarto Group,
142 West 36th Street, 4th Floor,
New York, NY 10018, USA
(212) 779-4972
www.Quarto.com

Wellfleet Press titles are also available at
discount for retail, wholesale, promotional, and
bulk purchase. For details, contact the Special
Sales Manager by email at specialsales@quarto.
com or by mail at The Quarto Group, Attn:
Special Sales Manager, 100 Cummings Center
Suite 265D, Beverly, MA 01915 USA.

10 9 8 7 6 5 4 3 2 1

ISBN: 978-1-57715-411-2

Digital edition published in 2024
eISBN: 978-0-7603-8840-2

Library of Congress Control Number:
2023951030

Group Publisher: Rage Kindelsperger
Creative Director: Laura Drew
Senior Art Director: Marisa Kwek
Editorial Director: Erin Canning
Managing Editor: Cara Donaldson
Editor: Elizabeth You
Cover and Interior Design: Tara Long

Printed in China

This book provides general information on
various widely known and widely accepted
images that tend to evoke feelings of strength
and confidence. However, it should not be
relied upon as recommending or promoting
any specific diagnosis or method of treatment
for a particular condition, and it is not intended
as a substitute for medical advice or for direct
diagnosis and treatment of a medical condition
by a qualified physician. Readers who have
questions about a particular condition, possible
treatments for that condition, or possible
reactions from the condition or its treatment
should consult a physician or other qualified
healthcare professional.